"Riley's book contains some great information on self-motivation techniques and ways to enhance one's health and longevity. It gives some excellent examples of how the sports metaphor can be applied to other areas in one's life."

— **Sally Edwards** —
President of Fleet Feet

"As a professional athlete it is easy to lose perspective of the larger picture. Single mindedness of purpose often leads to a one-dimensional life. *Designing Quality and Balance Into Your Life, Work, and Play* helped to remind me of the importance and benefits of living a balanced life!"

— **Dean Harper** —
World Class Professional Triathlete

"I most appreciated the motivation techniques and the balance you brought with your perspective on the need for both active work and active leisure. Encouraging people to strive for balance in their lives is not only a long term investment in personal success, it reflects a humane view of human need!"

— **John O. Najarian** —
President, K/P Graphics

"As an ambitious female, my life tends to get skewed toward professional pursuits to the demise of my personal and health interests. Riley's methods in *Designing Quality & Balance Into Your Life, Work and Play* work for me because they are practical and quantifiable. His check-list and tracking techniques help me keep focused on my career without neglecting other objectives that are important in balancing out my life."

— **Judy Finley** —
Director of Sales, Informatics General Corp.

Designing
Quality & Balance
Into Your Life, Work,
and Play

Jack Riley

Wilderness Press

Design by Thomas Winnett
Cover design by Tom Ridge
International Standard Book Number 0-89997-077-X
Manufactured in the United States of America
Published by Wilderness Press
          2440 Bancroft Way
          Berkeley, CA 94704

     Write for free catalog

Acknowledgements

My personal education and transformation were advanced by more people than I can credit here, but some of the most important have been: In work: Dick Tarrant, my ex-manager at IBM. In economics: my parents and my wife, LaVerne. In leisure: Jan Gault, Ph.D., Uptime; Dennis Young, California Peddler; Kerry O'Brien, Walnut Creek Masters swim coach. Relationships: my kids, Bob, Rick, Kathy, and Nancy. Spiritual: Monsignor Julius Bensen, formerly of St. Isidores parish, Danville, California; Carol Ruth Knox, Unity Church. Purpose: Bill Hackett and John Stanford, former Deans of Business, John F. Kennedy University; Keith McConnell, Associate Dean of Graduate Psychology Program, John F. Kennedy University. And finally I would like to thank Tom Winnett of Wilderness Press, who believed in my material and helped present it to a national audience.

I would also like to express my heartfelt appreciation for the encouragement and enthusiastic feedback given me by the students at John F. Kennedy University who took my seminar on Balance in Life and Work, and who convinced me that this material had such a significant impact on their lives that I should turn it into a book.

———————————— ♣ ————————————

Contents

Ch. 8 PURPOSE. 97

What motivates you to get out of bed in the morning? If you have ever wondered about the meaning of your life, this self-assessment will focus your sense of purpose and clarify your own intentions so that you can consciously work toward achieving them. In a balanced life, the five other areas fit comfortably within overall purpose.

Ch. 9 BALANCE IN LIFE, WORK AND PLAY. 105

Now you can put it all together. The quality-of-life action planner takes all your own, unique answers and puts them together in a way you can use most practically. Implementing your plan can be exciting and will be the key to a quality life.

Chapter 1

GET READY

Because of circumstance or personal crisis you have reached a fork in the path of your life. You have a choice: You can continue living as you have before, or you can decide to make a turn toward something better. This may be the most important decision you ever make, more important than your original career choice, or the choice you made when you married.

You are to be congratulated. Most people never even realize they have choices. But knowing you want to change is just the first step. Once considered, the possibilities seem infinite. Where should you begin? How can you know that the new direction will be any better than the old one? How does one go about creating a better way?

It's exciting to become aware that you can set forth on this new journey, and this book will show you how to do it, by investigating your own values, interests, and practices, and developing a step-by-step plan that is uniquely yours. This plan will meet your needs and further your ends because it uses your own personal talents and qualities as a foundation. Nothing less will do.

As we go along, I will be telling you a lot about myself because our subject matter is the most personal kind of subject matter and there is no other way to talk about it. This is real life we are talking about here, the nitty gritty. Some of mine isn't anything to brag about, and some of it is inspiring enough to bring tears to the eyes of the susceptible. But it is all true, because I knew when I put these ideas together that anything less than total honesty wouldn't work. These methods require the naked truth about ourselves.

I see the material in this book as an artist would see a painting or an architect would look at a cathedral he or she had created. This material is something I have created, and one of the purposes of my life is to present it to you. It came from my childhood, from my MBA program at the University of Chicago, from the many IBM management schools I attended, from a study of religions I made during my spiritual search, from Dr. George Sheehan's ideas on running and aerobics. It also came from Heartwood College of the Healing Arts in northern California, from Abraham Maslow, the noted psychologist, and from hundreds of other sources. We all have sources like these, sources which determine our perceptions and our outlook on life.

Last summer at the Montclair Art Show in Oakland, California I met an artist. He was a grey-bearded fellow with a piece of art not like anything I had ever seen before. It was metallic, and had very interesting colors. I stood and looked at it for a while, and then I asked him,

"How long did it take you to do that?"

He said, "Sixty years."

"No," I said, "I mean this piece of art right here. How long did it take you to do that?"

And he said again, "Sixty years."

Then I realized what he meant. It really did take all of his experience and skill development over a lifetime to get to the point where he could create that piece of art.

The book you hold in your hands is a piece of creativity of the same kind. It represents almost everything I have learned during my life, all the things that have made me who I am.

My personal renaissance began when I went to an eye doctor at the age of 47. At the time I was not feeling good. I was 5'8", 180 pounds, and had a very high cholesterol level and high blood pressure. I was starting to go downhill, but I hadn't faced my condition. I was having my glasses refitted and my eyes tested. The doctor looked into my eyes and said,

"Do you have a high cholesterol problem?"

I thought to myself, "How does he know that? He's an eye doctor." So I asked him, and he said,

"I can see the cholesterol coming out in your eye. There is a ring around the pupil that is a telltale sign."

That really scared me. It was the final, convincing point in a long series of messages and nudges the world had been giving me about the direction my life was going. I will tell you about the process I went through and how I created the method this book outlines, but first I want you to know what the method has done for me:

My life is at its highest quality level ever—at the age of 54—and it is getting better all the time. I won 25 triathlon medals in 1983, and was rated sixth in the country in the U.S. Triathlon Series Champion meet that year in my age division. In 1984 I was notified that I had set a world's athletic record at age 52 for the most triathlons in one year—52. That accomplishment is now recorded in *The Guinness Book of World Records.*

At age 52 also, I became vice president and general manager of a high-tech firm, and performed successfully, leading it to a 770% business increase, growing from $1.5 million to over $11 million in *one* year! Although I was the oldest employee, I had the lowest blood pressure of anyone in the company at the time. Then I started my own business— CHAPS, Corporate Health and Productivity Services. The intent of CHAPS is to help companies improve the quality of work life offered to their employees. We set up wellness and productivity programs. One company's program was so successful that I was asked to become a part owner and to help run the company on a day-to-day basis. In *four* months we increased sales *200%.* I was recently appointed to the board of advisors of a local university. My relationships are at their best level ever. Economically, I am closing in on the one-million-dollar net worth level.

I have begun to achieve my life purpose.

The philosophy I have developed is important to me because it keeps me growing. For many years, I had followed the path that society had programmed for me—until I finally said, "I don't have to let that happen to me." Now I keep an openness to new things. I think it is important, as we get older, to always be a rookie in something. I think that if you get too set in your ways, your world just keeps shrinking. I've watched many people narrow their lives as they grew older. They seem to narrow down, have less curiosity, do less seeking and searching. I saw my dad, who I thought was a great guy, go through that. In the end, for him, to go get the mail was a big thing in the morning, and to take a walk around the back yard was a big thing in the afternoon. That was it, that was his day. It was painful to watch.

Not only can this process involve narrowing, but it also can cause what I call Nixonism, where you feel you have it all together, and you can now set your own rules. I never want to feel so comfortable that that could happen. I want to have a quality life, all the way through.

I assume you do, too, or you wouldn't be looking for new directions on your road of life.

Today my life is balanced, and I have many achievements and many gratifications in many areas. But it wasn't always that way. For nearly 35 years, my life was just work and finances. That was all I had in life. I used to look at net worth only in financial terms. Now when I look at it, I ask, "What is my *true* net worth? I am a whole person. My net worth is the sum of my relationships, my spirituality, my leisure time, my purpose in life, my work, and my economic condition." You can see I look at net worth a lot differently now.

When I decided to do something about myself, I first thought only in terms of getting back into physical condition. I wanted to combat what was happening to my health. I had always been in shape as a young man, and fitness had always been important to me, but I had let myself get out of shape because my work was my life.

As a result of my experience with the eye doctor, and at the request of another doctor, I began running. Then I moved on to distance running. Then leisure—fitness—became my whole life. My work started to suffer, my family relationships started to suffer, as I put every thought and every effort into running.

But once I consistently devoted myself to the running, my whole body started to change. My vitality, my circulatory system, my chemistry began to change me into a different person. I woke up and became truly alive! This blossoming can happen to anyone at any age if they will allow it.

I began to have a lot more confidence, to be my own person more than I ever had been before. But this was all not without problems. Often people run because they are experiencing pain, or they are failing at something, and the running is an outlet. It can be a magnificent outlet, but my wife couldn't understand what in the world was happening to me, and we started to drift apart. At work I was a lot more confident, and a lot harder for my superiors to control.

So in the beginning of my pursuit of fitness there were many adjustment problems. After I let go of the total focus on work and went to the other extreme, where my whole life was running and was devoted to what you might call leisure, things were just as out of balance as they had always been. But in the end the change was very good for me all the way around, for running was the bridge that helped me eventually reach the balance I have now. I got out of a bad work environment and into a job where I own part of the company, my wife has also blossomed, my relationships with my four kids are great, and I'm in the best physical shape of my life.

As time went on, my outlook broadened, and I eventually understood that I could define my life as existing in six areas.

1. *Work,* which takes most of my waking day, and has for the last 30 years.

2. *Economics,* or finance, the part of life in which you ensure the financial capability to meet your needs.

3. *Leisure,* which is the time outside of work during which you choose what you will do.

4. *Relationships,* which have to do with the people you care about and who care about you.

5. *Spirituality,* which has to do with your inner self and how you relate to the universe.

6. *Purpose,* which gives your life its overall direction and meaning.

That is now my perception of the areas of my life.

On the next page you can draw your perception of your life, just as I have drawn mine as it used to be. What is the shape? Is it a circle? A pyramid? It doesn't really matter, so long as it's a shape that's congenial for you. How big are those various slices of the pie for you, or the levels of your pyramid? When you have decided on the shape, divide the figure up according to the amount of life energy you devote to each area. This is a picture, now, of how your life looks. Look at it. Is it the way you want it to be? Maybe not, or you wouldn't be reading this book. Now redraw the graphic figure as you would like your life to be. Size the slices or the levels according to how you would like to allocate your life energy. This is the first step in designing more quality (as you define it) into your new and expanded life. In my New Life figure you can see that the areas are more nearly equal. Even though I am physically at work 8 hours a day, I integrate Leisure (example: swimming at lunchtime), Relationships (example: building more quality in my relationships with my peers), Spiritual (example: taking meditation breaks), and Purpose (example: by the new work that I do) into the day. It gives me a much higher energy level and I am more productive and happy than I was. If you can't complete your graphic figure keep coming back to it as you are working on the exercises and you will eventually complete it.

The next step is to start thinking about what you want that you don't have, how you want things to be instead of the way they are. On the following page, write down what you are searching for in reading this book. What are the key things you want to get out of this book?

Some possibilities are: You are going through a transformation in your life and you want to set new goals. Or you want to understand yourself better, or to figure out why you have the kind of relationships you have. Maybe you are entering a new relationship and want to create new patterns of living with your new partner. Or you want to have more quality—or more balance—in your life. Perhaps you want to learn how to put motivation to work in your life, or to have more control. Or you may want to restructure your life entirely, from the foundation up.

How it was for me
(before)

How I wanted it to be
(and it is now)

Your life now   How you want it to be

What I'm Searching for in Reading This Book

I have presented this material in the form of a seminar many times, and people who have taken it have indicated all the purposes I've listed in the last paragraph, and more. They are searching for life direction, wanting to develop a new perspective, looking for peaks of experience, and wanting to know how to get there; they want to have a more fulfilling lifestyle, they want to learn how to prioritize the parts of their lives, or to integrate the various parts of the life they are living. It is vital at this stage to define what you want, so that you can create a plan, or strategy, for getting it.

Now, let's start your journey. Picture yourself as a sailor who wants to get from one shore to another. You are going across the lake of life, traveling from Painsville to Joysville. What affects that journey? Some things are the wind, the currents, time available, your skill, others' expectations of you, and the motivation that drives you. Isn't it interesting that so many of these are intangible, and yet they affect your ability to get to the other side.

Keeping in mind what your own goals are, then, list on the next page the things that must be considered to help you move toward them. Some possible things you might list are:
—support of your partner
—limited amount of money
—unwillingness to accept anything short of success
—importance placed on material things
—needs of your children. You get the idea.

How well we plan is the initial key to reaching our goal. When I worked for IBM, one of the things we always talked about was the need to plan the work, and then work the plan. For example, think about the first rocket the U.S. sent to the moon. Thousands of hours were spent planning the mission, but during flight that rocket was off course more than ninety percent of the time. However, there was a plan, a very detailed one, and the flight controllers worked the plan, making constant readjustments because there were so many unforeseen factors. They had to make small corrections, many *small steps,* to reach the desired target. Thus, even though for more than ninety percent of the time they were actually off course, they kept adjusting, and they landed exactly where they wanted to.

List of Considerations Necessary While Moving Toward Your Goal

The lesson is that what is needed to get where we are going, even when we are off course, is to take *small steps*. You may fail at certain times or parts of your life. We all do. But if you really understand who you are, you can use your interests and your talents to take small steps that will do the most good. It takes *small steps* and motivation, or inner drive. According to psychologist Abraham Maslow, you need to fully understand your inner drive and your capabilities so you can actualize your full potential.

For example, when I was a kid I always wanted to play football. But I was so small and light that the idea was ridiculous. I had to put books in my pants just to make the required weight for the lightweight team. And I was cut from the basketball team because I was too short. I was always trying to do these traditional things without looking at who and what I was. Most kids don't understand how to assess their own strong points and make the most of them. Many adults have the same problem.

The purpose of this book is to show you how to assess your own values, interests, and talents, and then to make the changes in your life that you want to make. Now and then throughout the book I'll be on my soapbox about fitness and athletics. I think they are extremely important, and I hope you do, too. But even if you have absolutely no interest in physical activity and never will, this is still the right book for you to use in reexamining your goals and reshaping your life. You can do the whole job sitting down!

Putting it simply, the object of this book is for you to go through a series of self-investigations to choose what you would *like to be doing,* measuring it against what you *are actually doing,* and set goals for yourself so that those two things will eventually match. The results will be more control over what happens to you, more joy out of life, more energy, and more self-actualization.

I want to salute you, you who are about to take your lives into your own hands and make of them what you want. Because I am revealing myself, I hope you will be motivated to be very honest with yourself, too. I have opened myself up, and I ask you to look forward to the experience of opening yourself up in your self-evaluation. My role as author is as a facilitator. I don't consider myself an expert in any of these areas of life, but my life has become a lot more balanced and happier as a result of experiencing the things you will read about here.

Without doubt, you will benefit from doing the exercises in the book. When you look back, perhaps six months after working through this material, you will have more of what you want out of life, and you will have reached your new stage through a series of *small steps,* almost painlessly.

Amost everyone who has ever attended one of the seminars upon which this book is based has told me that it had a significant impact on their life. I hope it will do the same for you.

Chapter 2

GET SET, GO

The starting point in balancing our lives is to learn who we are and what we want out of life. We are so bombarded with outside stimuli and so pressured to keep up the pace of society that we seldom take the time to try to understand ourselves.

With that idea in mind, I'd like you to think about your own life. Who are you? What are your unique values? What is important to you?

This chapter contains two techniques for quantification that will help you answer those questions. These techniques are the basis for the rest of the book. I have included copies of my own answers to the questions that I ask you to answer, both so you can learn more about me, and so you will have a practical guideline in understanding how the methods work.

The first self-assessment you will make is what I call the "Values Clarification." It begins on page 15. You will see that it is a list of values or qualities that people might choose to think are important. The values included on this list are not all the values you might hold dear, and if some things that are important to you are not on the list, add them at the bottom and include them in your assessment.

To fill out the form, read each item. Think about it. How important is it to you? Is it something you never think about? Something crucial? A quality you might only find amusing in another person? If it has no importance to you, rate it a 1, and write that number in the column headed "Importance" opposite the quality you are considering. If it is extremely important to you, rate it a 10, and write that number there. If it is of "average" importance, whatever that means to you, rate it a 5.

This "1–10" rating scale is the one used for most of the personal assessment forms in this book.

Begin now and take as much time as you need. It is very important for your success in this investigation that you be honest with yourself. Look at this as a measure of who you are today, not who your parents want you to be, who your husband or wife thinks you ought to be, but who you really are. Total self-honesty here is critical in setting the stage for the rest of the book. Otherwise you will only be kidding yourself as you go through the rest, and there will be no point in doing it.

If you have any questions about how to do this, take a look at my own "Values Clarification" on the page following the blanks. You will notice that there are two blank copies of this form, and a page from mine. Of the blank ones, one is for use now and the other for later—or for your partner.

When you have given a measure of importance to each of the values listed, go back and pick out the values you gave the highest scores to. Now rank them in importance. Take a look at mine. You will see that I gave Health a score of 10, Competitiveness 9, and Adventure 8. Economic Security, Freedom, Friendship, Personal Development, and Recognition also all had a score of 8. So I ranked Health as most important, and called it '1' in the rank column. Competitiveness was '2', and then I had to choose among the others for the '3' through '8' ranks.

Do this for yourself now. When you are through, read the instructions from beginning to end again and double-check that you are sure of what you did. This investigation is the foundation, remember, for the rest of the book. You want to be certain that you have been accurate.

And please, be honest with yourself. No one else ever needs to see this. A small embarrassment you might feel in the privacy of your own mind is of no importance compared to the damage you could do yourself and your future by *not* being honest. If Recognition is the most important thing to you, *give it a 1* in the ratings.

Values Clarification

Personal Values	Impor-tance	Rank Your Top 10
ACHIEVEMENT (a sense of accomplishment, mastery)		
ADVANCEMENT (promotion within a structure)		
ADVENTURE (new and challenging experiences)		
BEAUTY (making, appreciating or collecting it)		
COMFORT (on the physical level)		
COMPETENCE (doing things very well)		
COMPETITIVENESS (striving to win)		
CONTROL (making things happen exactly as you want)		
COOPERATION (working with others, teamwork)		
COSMIC PURPOSE (meaningful life)		
CREATIVITY (being imaginative, innovative, solving problems)		
ECONOMIC SECURITY (freedom from money worries)		
EQUALITY (personal and/or political)		
FAME (celebrity, known by public)		
FAMILY LIFE (personal gratifications from it)		
FREEDOM (independence, autonomy)		
FRIENDSHIP (mutually caring, close relationships)		
HAPPINESS (and the pursuit of it)		
HARMONY (peace with oneself and others)		
HEALTH (physical and mental well-being)		
HELPFULNESS (assisting others, improving society, kindness)		
HUMOR (laughing at self and the world, a sense of the ridiculous)		
INTEGRITY (honesty, sincerity, standing up for beliefs)		

Personal Values	Impor-tance	Rank Your Top 10
INVOLVEMENT (participation in larger cause, belonging with others)		
KNOWLEDGE (and the search for truth)		
LOVE (giving and receiving affection and caring)		
LOYALTY (duty, respectfulness, fidelity, constancy)		
MODERATION (temperance, lack of excess)		
MORALITY (ethical values)		
OBEDIENCE (compliance, dutifulness)		
ORDER (stability, unchangingness)		
PERSONAL DEVELOPMENT (use of potential)		
PLEASURE (carefree enjoyment, fun)		
PRESERVATION (conservatism, keeping valuable things)		
POWER (over people or conditions)		
REBELLION (opposition to authority, revolt)		
RECOGNITION (being recognized as someone important)		
SPIRITUAL (of the spirit, soul, higher mind)		
RESPONSIBILITY (being accountable, dependable)		
RISK TAKING (excitement of confronting changing conditions)		
SALVATION (saving of the soul)		
SELF-RESPECT (self-esteem)		
STATUS (position of high public standing)		
SOCIAL CONCERN (making a better world for people)		
WEALTH (riches)		
INTELLECTUAL STIMULATION (sharing intellectual energy)		
QUALITY (the degree of excellence)		
UNITY (oneness)		

Personal Values	Impor-tance	Rank Your Top 10
STABILITY (steadiness)		
Add your own:		

Values Clarification

Personal Values	Impor-tance	Rank Your Top 10
ACHIEVEMENT (a sense of accomplishment, mastery)		
ADVANCEMENT (promotion within a structure)		
ADVENTURE (new and challenging experiences)		
BEAUTY (making, appreciating or collecting it)		
COMFORT (on the physical level)		
COMPETENCE (doing things very well)		
COMPETITIVENESS (striving to win)		
CONTROL (making things happen exactly as you want)		
COOPERATION (working with others, teamwork)		
COSMIC PURPOSE (meaningful life)		
CREATIVITY (being imaginative, innovative, solving problems)		
ECONOMIC SECURITY (freedom from money worries)		
EQUALITY (personal and/or political)		
FAME (celebrity, known by public)		
FAMILY LIFE (personal gratifications from it)		
FREEDOM (independence, autonomy)		
FRIENDSHIP (mutually caring, close relationships)		
HAPPINESS (and the pursuit of it)		
HARMONY (peace with oneself and others)		
HEALTH (physical and mental well-being)		
HELPFULNESS (assisting others, improving society, kindness)		
HUMOR (laughing at self and the world, a sense of the ridiculous)		
INTEGRITY (honesty, sincerity, standing up for beliefs)		

Personal Values	Impor-tance	Rank Your Top 10
INVOLVEMENT (participation in larger cause, belonging with others)		
KNOWLEDGE (and the search for truth)		
LOVE (giving and receiving affection and caring)		
LOYALTY (duty, respectfulness, fidelity, constancy)		
MODERATION (temperance, lack of excess)		
MORALITY (ethical values)		
OBEDIENCE (compliance, dutifulness)		
ORDER (stability, unchangingness)		
PERSONAL DEVELOPMENT (use of potential)		
PLEASURE (carefree enjoyment, fun)		
PRESERVATION (conservatism, keeping valuable things)		
POWER (over people or conditions)		
REBELLION (opposition to authority, revolt)		
RECOGNITION (being recognized as someone important)		
SPIRITUAL (of the spirit, soul, higher mind)		
RESPONSIBILITY (being accountable, dependable)		
RISK TAKING (excitement of confronting changing conditions)		
SALVATION (saving of the soul)		
SELF-RESPECT (self-esteem)		
STATUS (position of high public standing)		
SOCIAL CONCERN (making a better world for people)		
WEALTH (riches)		
INTELLECTUAL STIMULATION (sharing intellectual energy)		
QUALITY (the degree of excellence)		
UNITY (oneness)		

Personal Values	Impor-tance	Rank Your Top 10
STABILITY (steadiness)		
Add your own:		

Author's Values Clarification

Personal Values	Impor-tance	Rank Your Top 10
ACHIEVEMENT (a sense of accomplishment, mastery)	5	
ADVANCEMENT (promotion within a structure)	2	
ADVENTURE (new and challenging experiences)	8	3
BEAUTY (making, appreciating or collecting it)	4	
COMFORT (on the physical level)	3	
COMPETENCE (doing things very well)	7	
COMPETITIVENESS (striving to win)	9	2
CONTROL (making things happen exactly as you want)	6	
COOPERATION (working with others, teamwork)	5	
COSMIC PURPOSE (meaningful life)	6	
CREATIVITY (being imaginative, innovative, solving problems)	7	
ECONOMIC SECURITY (freedom from money worries)	8	4
EQUALITY (personal and/or political)	6	
FAME (celebrity, known by public)	5	
FAMILY LIFE (personal gratifications from it)	7	
FREEDOM (independence, autonomy)	8	5
FRIENDSHIP (mutually caring, close relationships)	8	6
HAPPINESS (and the pursuit of it)	6	
HARMONY (peace with oneself and others)	6	
HEALTH (physical and mental well-being)	10	1
HELPFULNESS (assisting others, improving society, kindness)	7	
HUMOR (laughing at self and the world, a sense of the ridiculous)	5	
INTEGRITY (honesty, sincerity, standing up for beliefs)	7	

As you can see from my Values Clarification, I like competition a lot. In a business environment I'm a Type A. That is the way I approached my business tasks in the past. What I am doing now is balancing my life so I don't stifle my competitiveness, but allow it to come into play, and enjoy it in the proper situations. I am a very physical person, and athletic competition is very gratifying to me. As a very goal-oriented person, running or biking or swimming or whatever, I want to win. But when it is over, I like to have a beer with the people I've been competing with. We have fun then, too.

Adventure is my third most important value. Triathlons are great adventures. The terrain and the difficulties are always unknowns. But you will see that for me Economic Security is #4. So here's a balance again. Freedom, Friendship, and Personal Development come next. And Recognition: That's part of why I do these athletic things, too. I like recognition. I used to feel guilty about that. But that is me. I need to have ways of being recognized. Love and Spiritual are also in my top ten values.

The second form you will fill out, on the following page, is the "Quality of Life Matrix." This will give you a status report on where you are in your life now, based on the values that are most important to you, as you have just now identified them. I have taken the business concept of accounting and applied it to balancing life, in a unique way.

To fill out the Matrix, transfer the values from the Clarification to the column on the left side of the Matrix labeled Top Ten Values. You can take a look at my example as a guide. List them in descending importance, with the most important at the top.

Now look at your values, one at a time, in relationship to the six areas of life spaced across from left to right. As an example, if Achievement is your most important value, ask yourself, on a scale of 1 to 10, how actualized that value is in your work environment. Are you able to get a sense of accomplishment from work? If the answer is yes, put down a 9 or 10 in the row to the right of the word "Achievement," and under the column headed "Work." But if you don't get that feeling from work, if you can't get your ideas implemented and you always seem to be behind in achieving anything at work, rate yourself just a 2 or 3 there.

Quality of Life Matrix

Areas of Life

Top Ten Values (Transferred from your values clarification)	WORK	ECONOMIC	LEISURE	RELATIONSHIP	SPIRITUAL	PURPOSE	TOTALS	RANK
1.								
2.								
3.								
4.								
5.								
6.								
7.								
8.								
9.								
10.								
Area of Life Totals								
Rank								

Author's Quality of Life Matrix

Areas of Life

Top Ten Values (Transferred from your values clarification)	WORK	ECONOMIC	LEISURE	RELATIONSHIP	SPIRITUAL	PURPOSE	TOTALS	RANK
1. Health	5	5	10	7	2	7	36	5
2. Competitiveness	5	5	10	5	5	9	39	6
3. Adventure	5	5	9	8	7	8	42	2
4. Security	9	5	5	3	5	6	36	9
5. Freedom	7	8	8	8	7	8	46	1
6. Friendship	6	5	7	8	6	9	41	3/4
7. Personal Development	4	6	7	7	8	9	41	3/4
8. Recognition	4	7	9	6	5	7	38	8
9. Love	4	5	8	9	7	5	38	7
10. Spiritual	2	5	7	6	7	7	34	10
Area of Life Totals	51	59	80	67	59	75	391	
Rank	6	4/5	1	3	4/5	2		

♣

Then consider your value of Achievement in terms of the economic area of your life. How much have you been financially rewarded for your achievements? Would you rate yourself there as a 3, a 7, or what? Fill in that box. Keep referring to my example to help get the feel of this important exercise. If there are a few values that don't seem to "fit" in a particular area of life, just give them a 5. For example, I did that on my form for the value "Competitiveness" in the Spiritual area. When a value has a 5, it has almost a neutral effect on the outcome.

Do the same with each of the columns, moving across from left to right opposite the value of Achievement (or whatever your first value is). Are your leisure activities promoting your sense of Achievement? How much feeling of accomplishment do you get from your relationships? Rate yourself there, too. Do the same with the Spiritual and Purpose columns. If you feel you need more clarification, refer to the definitions of the areas of life on page 5. If you still have a question about any of the six areas of life, turn ahead to the chapter on it and read the first page or two.

Now do the same thing with each of your other nine top values. Don't hurry. If you don't have time to finish this now, come back to it later. Take the time to give it care. This matters—a lot.

When you have filled in all the boxes under the six areas of life, add up your scores from top to bottom in each column. The totals you get will tell you which areas of life are fulfilling your own values best. You can rate them in order of the amount of fulfillment they give you. If the Relationship column total is the biggest, then you can see right there that, quantified by your own standards, your relationships give you more fulfillment than any other area of your life.

A low score shows you which areas of life aren't giving you the fulfillment you might have.

Then add up the rows horizontally: Total the scores for each value across the page. Then determine the highest scoring value of all the horizontal sums, and rate it 1. Find the lowest score and rate it 10, and fill in the scores of each of the others. This will tell you which of your values are being fulfilled and which are not. Review my example if you need to clarify how to do this.

You will probably find that the order you end up with is not the same as your conscious priorities. That is, your highest value will not be the one with the highest score in the "Totals" column, and your lowest will not be number 10 on the list. For example, my highest actual score was for Freedom, but I had listed it as the fifth most important value to me. And my highest value, Health, was exceeded in score by four other values.

People look at life differently, and your quantifications will not be the same as anyone else's. But unless you are severely depressed or extremely elated when you take these self-examinations, you are likely to use the same quantifying standards each time you take them. So the changes you find when you take them again will be objective.

The Quality of Life Matrix is a status report to yourself on how well you've been running your life. It also shows you where you might want to make changes.

There are no right or wrong scores. This is not an issue for judgment. If you are very high in one area, great! You may know more about that area than I can tell you in this book. If so, drop me a line and give me some of your ideas.

If you are low in an area, maybe you will want to pay particular attention to the chapter on that area which follows. It will give you ideas and some ways to take action to improve your score in that part of your life. Another technique for doing this exercise is one that people in my seminars have used: Several people—each one with his own book—work together, sharing their ideas and doing the exercise together. In fact, this technique is both enjoyable and effective for doing any exercise in this book.

This simple pair of personal clarifications will give you a very clear picture of what is *really* going on in your life.

After I first filled out the Work Values column in the Quality of Life Matrix, I worked with my boss to enhance my job. Eventually, I changed jobs. I could see that I would be happier, and I was right. I'm so much better off now. My original score on Work Values was 51. Now it is 74. So that is almost a 50% improvement in how I feel about my work. Fantastic!

Seeing my values and how well they are being fulfilled on paper like that was illuminating. People who take my seminar say, "I've never been able to look at my life that way, to quantify it." This paper exercise lets you see how the different areas of your life affect the wholeness of it, and how you can do something to increase your overall well-being.

When you have completed the Quality of Life Matrix, you are ready to begin dealing with the individual areas of your life. Each of the chapters that follow covers one of the six areas of living: Work, Economics, Leisure, Relationships, Spirituality, and Purpose.

For best results, do each section in its entirety in one sitting. You may do one or three or all six chapters at one time, but don't stop in the middle of one. And it would be better if you could avoid interruption, so time your investigations for moments when you expect to be alone. This is very important work you will be doing, and it deserves your undivided attention.

It is your story, your opportunity to enhance your uniqueness. Are you willing to be truly alive?

GO FOR IT!

Chapter 3

WORKING

If true balance is our intention,
Then work is but one dimension.

Just as we all have certain unique values in life, in work we have unique skills and interests. That is what I will be talking about in this chapter.

I once heard Bernie Haldane, of Haldane and Associates, speak. Haldane has a psychology background, and psychology is the essence of his company. When he gets a new client— someone looking for a job—one of the first orders of business is a battery of tests. One of the most important, so far as Haldane is concerned, is the test that determines what the person's "dependable skills" are. Haldane says that if a person is matched up with a job in which they are utilizing their dependable skills, then automatically their job stress level will be less.

Haldane looks at the key skills of a person and tries to fit them into an appropriate type of work. For example, consider a carpenter who has had years of working with his hands and has developed his skills to a high degree. He loves and takes pride in his craftsmanship. Then he becomes a contractor, and assumes administrative responsibilities. He may be an adequate administrator, but the demands of that job do not call for his truly dependable skills. So for him, automatically, there is more stress in doing those administrative tasks than in hammering nails, carving wood, and so on.

———————— ♣ ————————

A salesperson, for another example, may love talking to people, motivating others, competing in the market. If he becomes vice president and spends his time making policy, doing budgets, and hiring and firing people, he may find he hates it.

One person who painted billboards on barns said that the secret of life is to figure out what you really love to do, and then get someone to pay you for doing it. Recently when I was being filmed for a health video while running a treadmill, I remembered that quote and it gave me a very warm feeling.

So it is important to find out what your most dependable skills are. Haldane says that one way to do this is to close your eyes, sit back, and remember your youth. Think of the experiences you had that you were most proud of, things that you did well, that really turned you on or made you feel the happiest. And think about the people you liked or respected and who influenced you the most.

On the next blank page, write down what those experiences were and who those people were.

When I did this, I found that I really liked motivating people and doing some marketing things—selling and planning how to make sales—and that the one person I really looked up to was a salesman who worked for my dad. I thought he was the neatest guy. I liked his personality, the way he handled people, and the results he got. We would make calls together on builders in the Watchung Mountains in New Jersey. I also loved being outdoors. I hadn't even realized until I did this exercise how much that man had impressed me, but he had quite a lasting influence on me.

As I thought about the question more, I recalled a coach I really liked, and how he handled the boys. And I realized just how important the trinkets, the little medals I won for physical achievements at the YMCA, were to me. I still have them in my den.

Now look at your list. Are some of those pleasant experiences incorporated in your present work? Are you doing those kinds of activities; do you have those kinds of people around you? I find that only 10% of the people in an audience can say

Experiences I was most proud of, that I did well and that really turned me on:

People who influenced me the most:

yes; 90% of the people have not allowed that extra potential happiness into their lives.

Because most people spend more than 50% of their waking hours at work, it is important to match up your dependable skills with what you are doing in your work if you want to minimize stress. That is one of the ways balance in work life is achieved.

I have been working since high school—some 35 years. When I look back on my working career, I'm amazed at the diversity of it. Just some of the things I've done are: selling Christmas cards; selling newspapers; developing a new local newspaper; writing and distributing the newspaper; common labor; truck driving; selling fuel oil; dispatching; and cutting lawns with a hand lawn mower. (I used to love the physical exertion of conquering a very high lawn that hadn't been cut for a long time. It was fun literally to mow it down. I think that was when I began to realize that I had a very physical nature.)

I was also a carpenter's apprentice, a fighter pilot in the U.S. Air Force, and then a Strategic Air Command pilot. I loved being a fighter pilot because it was competition. I loved the soaring up in the sky and the physical nature of it; it was like playing football or basketball or other team competition. But when I was transferred to the Strategic Air Command, my outlook was totally changed and I lost interest in staying in the Air Force. The reason was that my mission there, my responsibility, was to carry and drop, if necessary, a hydrogen bomb. I piloted a B-47 bomber, and my mission in response to a Soviet attack was to obliterate a city in the Vladivostok region of the Soviet Union. I got out of the service then, as fast as I could, because every day I was training to do something that I really did not want to do.

I was also a sales rep for IBM and for another company that sold hydroponic equipment; I was a hay broker, a marketing consultant, a manager, a coach, a rancher. I've had an opportunity to look at work and to be involved in a number of boring jobs that I didn't want at all, but did anyway, and also in many very actualizing forms of work.

One of the most important tools I have used in creating my success in work has been a habit of setting goals and planning how to get where I wanted to go. Let me give you an example of how this helped me, in a work environment, to go from a very average IBM salesperson to the top seller in the Midwest region in selling new accounts.

If there are two things that are required to be successful, in my humble opinion, they are a burning desire to succeed and good work habits. Selling at IBM was my first job after the Air Force. I was assigned initially to the Chicago office, but after a month they transferred me to Hammond, Indiana. I think I was probably evaluated at that point as the least likely to succeed, and being sent to Hammond from Chicago was like being sent to the farm club or the minor leagues.

After my new boss spent the first day with me, he said he was sorry they had sent me through training so quickly because it was obvious that I needed more training and would have more. Then he asked me what territory I would like. This was a steel and petrochemical area, so I said, "Well, John, I'd like the steel firms."

"Other than the steel firms, what would you like?" he asked.

"The petrochemical companies," I said.

"Ah, other than the petrochemical companies, what?"

It was pretty obvious how he was rating me. I said, "Well, John—what am I gonna get?"

And he said, "Kankakee, Illinois."

Kankakee was hardly the computer capital of the world at that time. However, when I left the territory five years later, there was an article in the paper—on the front page—calling Kankakee the most computerized small town in America. I was proud that I had made that happen.

At the time I was attending the University of Chicago at night, working for an MBA. While my wife was busy having and tending to four kids, I was for five years going to school at night. Part of the reason was to get out of the house and away from the screaming kids.

In a statistics class we applied statistics to our job as a case study. Vilfredo Pareto, whom we had just studied, intrigued me. He was an Italian economist at the turn of the century who analyzed who had the wealth in Rome. He found that 80% of the wealth was in the hands of 20% of the people. He also found that the same percentage breakdown carried over into many other areas of activity, and he developed what he called the 80/20 rule.

I myself had seen that rule apply in many areas: 20% of the salesmen sell 80% of the goods; 20% of the items in inventory have 80% of the dollar value; 20% of the outstanding accounts receivable represent 80% of the outstanding money due; 20% of the athletes win 80% of the medals, and on and on.

So I looked at my territory, applied the 80/20 rule, and started to allocate my time in the same proportions: I spent 80% of my time on the 20% of the prospects who were the best prospects. The rule helped me to determine where I would put my energy. Since then I've taken that rule and applied it to many other areas of my life. The rule is like a guide for determining return on investment (ROI) from invested energy.

Something else I learned in that statistics class was to quantify things more than I had in the past. One of the goals I had that year was to lead the Midwest region in selling to new accounts. My territory was definitely not the prime territory to do that in, but that was my goal at the beginning of the year. I wrote it down on paper and affirmed it daily.

My strategy was to take all the prospective accounts and rate them, quantifying the opportunity for sales. I used two scales.

One was potential. At that point the alternatives possible were to sell them a low-cost small punch-card system, a medium-cost punch-card system, or a higher-cost small computer. I would give the account three points if it was a higher-cost computer potential, two points for a medium-cost punch-card sales potential, and one for a low-cost punch-card system.

The other part of the analysis was the current interest level of the company. If it had a high degree of interest, I gave it a three, medium interest got a two, and low interest, one.

I went through all my prospects and added up the ratings of each. That showed me which accounts held the best opportunities for me. Each month I would spend 80% of my time on the top 20% of the opportunities. I was quantifying opportunities using Pareto's rule in planning my time.

That was my plan. I also had a self-evaluation. Many times we go through life implementing somebody else's plan, and waiting for someone else's evaluation. I think it's important to have one's own, not only in work, but in other areas of life too—especially when the rewards we seek are a long time coming, but we have need for frequent feedback.

When you're selling large computers, you don't sell one every day—particularly when you're new at it. It may be months before you make your first sale, as it was for me, and you can get very depressed. So it was important for me to develop a way that I could feel good about myself even when I wasn't making sales. I couldn't control when the sales would come, but I could control my activities. So I made myself a rating scale for my activities. I gave myself points for things I did. A phone call earned me one point, a personal call on a prospect earned two points, and so on.

I would go through the day accumulating points. I developed a standard for myself of how many points made a good, solid week. I set a goal for myself, and I would evaluate my performance at the end of the week. That was my way of following the slogan, "Plan your work, work your plan." It gave me a sense of accomplishments to be able to quantify my work. I call this goal-accounting or success-accounting.

It was fun. It was a game. I may have had weeks in which I didn't sell anything, and my boss may have wondered why I seemed to be so pleased with myself. My secret of good morale was my own evaluation system, which was objective and truthful. If my overall goal for the week was 100 points, and I made 125, I felt great. I could go out and celebrate Friday night. It was very helpful to me in maintaining my confidence.

By using these techniques, by having a strategy and a plan, and by hard work, I reached my goal: At the end of that year I was the top account salesperson in the Midwest region for selling the most new accounts.

I use this same technique in management and in my leisure athletic activities: breaking the whole down into pieces and then improving the pieces in small steps. The value of these methods has been proved to me again and again in many areas of my life.

The Work Preference Self-Analysis, which follows, will allow you to quantify what you enjoy and how often you are doing it in your work. Using a scale of 1 to 10, read the description of each work activity and think about how much you enjoy doing it. First go through the whole list, rating your enjoyment of each kind of work activity. See my sample and the rating scale below.

Once you have completed that, start at the beginning again in the "frequency" column, and ask yourself about each activity just how often you are actually doing it in your work, again using a scale of 1 to 10.

After completing that column, start again at the beginning and fill in the variances. If you rated yourself 8 on "Plant, Cultivate" in enjoyment, but in frequency you showed 2, then your variance is +6. This means that you like to do it, but your work life now is not allowing you to do it. Thus you are missing out on additional possible enjoyment and stress reduction in work.

If your enjoyment was 2, but the frequency was 8, your variance is −6, meaning that you don't like to do it, but your current work life requires it—automatically inducing more stress.

Go through each activity this way, entering the variances, plus or minus. When you are through, you will have a very good picture of what you like to do versus what you do—and a quantitative measure of the differences.

The large variances will be the ones to concentrate on. Think about those. If you are spending enough time transporting people or things to have marked your frequency as 6, but your enjoyment of it is 1, you can decide whether or not you want to keep on doing that. Isn't there an alternative?

On the other hand, if your frequency of entertaining/performing is 1, but you rated your enjoyment of it as 8, you might want to think about finding time to do some entertaining. If that requires talking to your boss about job enhancement, or getting another job, then do it. If you have to go outside of work to reduce this variance, you might join a little theater group, or become a freelance magician. In the "Action" column write what you could do to reduce the variance. Then take that first small action step in that direction.

Rating Scale

Enjoyment

1 Hate it.
2 Avoid opportunities actively.
3 Would be happy never to do it.
4 Occasionally pleasurable.
5 Average interest.
6 Really don't mind it at all.
7 Gladly include it.
8 Take real pleasure in doing it.
9 Actively look for opportunities.
10 Wonderful. Love it.

Frequency

1 Very rarely or never.
2 Very seldom.
3 Occasionally.
4 Once or twice a month.
5 Average frequency.
6 Fairly often.
7 With regularity.
8 Once a week or more.
9 Several times a week.
10 Every day or more.

This scale is just a guide. Adapt it to your own needs.

Work Preference Self-Analysis

Activity	Enjoyment (+)	Frequency (−)	Variance (+/−)	Action
ACT AS LIAISON— Represent, serve as a link between individuals or groups.				
ANALYZE— Break down, figure out problems logically.				
BUDGET— Economize, save, stretch money or other resources.				
CLASSIFY— Group, categorize, systematize data, people or things.				
COMPOSE MUSIC—Write & arrange music for voice or instruments.				
COUNSEL— Facilitate insight & personal growth; guide, advise, coach students, employees or clients.				
COUNT—Tally, calculate, compute quantities.				

Activity	Enjoyment (+)	Frequency (−)	Variance (+/−)	Action
DEAL WITH FEELINGS— Draw out, listen, accept, empathize, express sensitivity, defuse anger, calm, inject humor, appreciate people.				
DESIGN— Structure new or innovative practices, programs, products or environments.				
ENTERTAIN, PERFORM— Amuse, sing, dance, act, play music, give a demonstration, speak to an audience.				
ESTIMATE— Appraise value or cost of goods or services.				
EVALUATE— Assess, review, critique feasibility or quality.				
EXPEDITE— Speed up production or services, trouble-shoot problems, streamline procedures.				

Activity	Enjoyment (+)	Frequency (−)	Variance (+/−)	Action
GENERATE IDEAS—Conceive of, dream up, brainstorm, reflect upon ideas.				
HOST/HOSTESS —Make welcome, put at ease, provide comfort & pleasure, serve visitors, guests and customers.				
IMPLEMENT— Provide detailed follow-through of plans and policies.				
INITIATE CHANGE—Exert influence on changing the status quo, exercise leadership in bringing about new directions.				
INTERVIEW FOR INFORMA-TION—Draw out subjects through incisive questioning.				
MAINTAIN RECORDS— Keep accurate and up-to-date records, log, record, itemize, collate, tabulate data.				

Activity	Enjoyment (+)	Frequency (−)	Variance (+/−)	Action
MAKE ARRANGE- MENTS— Coordinate events, handle logistics of goods and people.				
MAKE DECI- SIONS—Make major, complex or frequent decisions.				
MEDIATE— Manage conflict, reconcile differences between people or groups.				
MONITOR— Keep track of the movement of data, people or things.				
MOTIVATE— Recruit involve- ment and mobilize energy, stimulate peak performance.				
NEGOTIATE— Bargain for rights or advantages.				
OBSERVE— Study, scrutinize, examine data, people or things scientifically.				
PERCEIVE INTUITIVELY— Sense, show insight and foresight.				

Activity	Enjoyment (+)	Frequency (−)	Variance (+/−)	Action
PLAN, ORGANIZE— Define goals & objectives, schedule & develop projects or programs.				
PLANT, CULTIVATE— Grow food, flowers, trees, lawns, prepare soil, plant, water, fertilize, weed, harvest, trim, prune, mow.				
PORTRAY IMAGES— Sketch, draw, illustrate, paint, and photograph.				
PREPARE FOOD—Wash, cut, bake and blend, arrange for nutrition, taste and aesthetics.				
PRODUCE SKILLED CRAFTS—Shape, weave, attach, etch, carve ornamental gift or display items.				
PROOFREAD, EDIT—Check writings for proper usage, content and style, make improvements.				

Activity	Enjoyment (+)	Frequency (−)	Variance (+/−)	Action
READ FOR INFORMATION —Research written resources efficiently & exhaustively.				
SELL—Promote a person, company, product or service, convince of merits and value, raise money.				
STAGE SHOWS— Produce theatrical, art, fashion or trade shows & other events for public performance or display.				
SUPERVISE— Oversee, direct the work of others.				
SYNTHESIZE— Integrate ideas & information, combine diverse elements into a coherent whole.				
TEACH, TRAIN—Inform, explain, give instruction to students, employees or customers.				

Activity	Enjoyment (+)	Frequency (−)	Variance (+/−)	Action
TEND ANIMALS— Feed, shelter, breed, train, show domestic pets, farm or ranch animals.				
TEST—Measure proficiency, quality or validity, check & double-check.				
TRANSPORT— Drive, lift, carry, haul.				
TREAT, NURSE—Heal, cure patients or clients.				
USE CARPENTRY ABILITIES— Construct, maintain or restore buildings, fittings or furnishings.				
USE MECHANICAL ABILITIES— Assemble, tune, repair or operate engines or other machinery.				
USE OTHER CONSTRUC- TIVE ABILI- TIES—Assemble, program or repair electronic equipment.				

Activity	Enjoyment (+)	Frequency (−)	Variance (+/−)	Action
USE PHYSICAL COORDINA- TION & AGILITY—Walk, run, climb, scale, jump, balance, aim, throw, catch or hit.				
VISUALIZE— Imagine possibilities, see in the mind's eye.				
WRITE—Com- pose reports, let- ters, articles, ads, stories, books or educational materials.				
(Other:)				

*This form adapted from the "Motivated Skills Card Sort" created by Richard Knowdell, copyright 1981, Career Research & Testing, San Jose, CA 95128.

Author's Work Preference Self-Analysis
(partial)

Activity	Enjoyment (+)	Frequency (−)	Variance (+/−)	Action
ACT AS LIAISON— Represent, serve as a link between individuals or groups.	4	6	-2	
ANALYZE— Break down, figure out problems logically.	3	6	-3	
BUDGET— Economize, save, stretch money or other resources.	3	6	-3	
CLASSIFY— Group, categorize, systematize data, people or things.	4	4	0	
COMPOSE MUSIC—Write & arrange music for voice or instruments.	2	2	0	
COUNSEL— Facilitate insight & personal growth; guide, advise, coach students, employees or clients.	8	5	+3	
COUNT—Tally, calculate, compute quantities.	3	5	-2	

Activity	Enjoyment (+)	Frequency (−)	Variance (+/−)	Action
DEAL WITH FEELINGS— Draw out, listen, accept, empathize, express sensitivity, defuse anger, calm, inject humor, appreciate people.	8	4	+4	Spend the time to better understand people's needs.
MOTIVATE— Recruit involvement and mobilize energy, stimulate peak performance.	9	5	+4	Develop a plan to promote wellness and balance in work groups.

You will notice that there is no mention of how well you do these things. You may love to sell, for example, but not consider yourself a good salesperson. What is important here is your desire, because if you really want to do something, you can learn how.

If you are maximizing your dependable skills, you will get there, even if it means "paying some dues." You may have to get some training; it may take some time. But you will be better off in the long run working at something you enjoy doing. It is one of the *keys* to a happy life.

Now look at your list. Does a pattern jump out at you? Can you see a way the listed activities fit together? If so, you have grasped something important about yourself.

Even if you don't see any pattern, take the next step: Write in an action for each of the activities with a significant variance. It can be something simple, like "less budgeting," or "more physical activity." Or you may want to think further ahead, and write in something like "star in local play." But be sure to write in some action for each activity with a significant variance.

Did you see *Fiddler on the Roof*? The fiddler was playing his tune, fiddling away, but also at the same time he was hanging onto the roof. You can see a job environment in that way. Many times you want to play your tune, but you're also just hanging onto the environment. You would like to spend 90% of your energy playing your tune, and only 10% having to hang onto the roof, or the work environment. But many times it is the other way around—10% and 90%.

Many people don't recognize until middle age—if ever— that they have been defining themselves in terms of their work. If you ask a man who he is, he is likely to tell you that he is a plumber, or an ad executive, or a statistical analyst. A woman these days probably will do the same, although she may instead say she is a housewife and/or a mother. Either way, the person is saying, "I am the work I do."

Do you feel good about the label you put on yourself? Because to some extent, this is true, we are what we do and, as my mother used to say, "We are who we associate with." That is why it is important to work at employment that offers enjoyment and gratification, and with people you respect and enjoy.

Many of the most unhappy people in middle age are those who have only that single source of self-esteem, which they have virtually beat to death. The older woman who reminds her family continually of the long-suffering care-giving she has provided will drive her family away from her. A man or woman who has put their whole life into their work will be devastated when they retire and people stop returning their phone calls.

But if your work is just a part of a balanced life, that won't happen. Life is bigger than just work, and you can't afford to get caught in the workaholic syndrome, even if you have a working environment that is totally enjoyable.

Chapter 4

ECONOMICS: PERSONAL

Just having money
Doesn't make one's life sunny.

Think: What is your economic situation?

To answer that question, I have for twenty years been using a very simple method that works. It is embodied in the form on page 56. It is a basic thing, like all the methods we've been talking about here; it is a way to keep score. Just as it was important for me to keep track of how I was doing in my job, I also keep score of my financial condition at the end of each year. Companies do it. We all do it to some extent, because when it is time to do our tax returns, we have to sit down and look at the past year and think about our financial situation. But most people just look at their records in order to find out how much taxes they owe. They don't look at their *net worth*. That is what I think is important. What is your net worth?

Using this method caused me to change from a relatively unhappy work situation I'd put 25 years into, to where I am today. I could have stayed with the company and mildewed and waited for retirement. But that's not what I wanted. That's awful. There's so much more to get out of life. There are so many more contributions I could make.

With the company, being a good employee meant putting the company first. To them, my performance was beside the point. The real reason for their dissatisfaction was my attitude.

After I was transferred to California, I spent two years here and knew I wanted to stay. But I was to be promoted to Detroit.

"Wait a minute," I said to myself. "Being here and doing what I do with my family is more important to me than being on that treadmill." "I'm not going to Detroit," I told them. And at that point I got off the career ladder. The company knows what that kind of insubordination means. To them it means, "Jack is not a career person."

Later I began to feel that the work was boring. They were not giving me any new challenges. I was not an exceller by their standards. After I refused the Detroit promotion, they stopped promoting me at all. I wanted to be promoted in the branch in California, but they said, "No, we don't do that. You have to move around." Then another person came in as manager, and even though I was loyal—too loyal—my motivation started to dwindle.

That was my big turning point. Now I feel sorry for the business people—male or female—who are really successful by the traditional corporate rules. They've never had a personal crisis that made them rethink their lives. If you're ever going to design your own life, you have to hit a crisis along the way that makes you reexamine your path. Are you going to keep your nose to it, or are you going to blossom out?

To get through a change, I had my own ideas and techniques to rely on. I also had support from the people around me; my family totally supported me. I told them, "I'm walking away from that." It was $40–50,000 a year, but I wasn't happy. After I left I spent three months redesigning my life. I had to get 25 years of business stress out of my system. My wife never once pushed or doubted me. Never once. She had raised the kids and gone back to work, yet while I was sitting around for three months she never said a word.

That kind of experience brings people closer together. I'm not even sure she knows how much I appreciate her for that. What her response told me was that she believed in me and understood what I was doing. My boss at work had told me that he didn't believe in me. We all like to feel that we are worthy, and that people believe in us.

I really am happy that I had the courage to change. After I joined a high-tech company, within six months I had hired a national sales force of 17 people. In one year we grew from $1.5 million in sales to over $11 million—a 770% increase. And I was promoted to general manager. So much for my not being a good sales manager.

I think it's good to have some disasters along the way. It's very good, no question about it—you learn more from failure than from success. Gail Sheehy says in *Pathfinders* that there are ten hallmarks of the pathfinder. One of them is that he or she has handled one or more serious transitions in their life and has been able to rebound from it. When you read the personal stories of outstanding people in history, like Winston Churchill, you find they've all had some very hard times along the way, but they have been able to rebound and recover.

It was very valuable to me to have been downgraded by my former company. The first thing I did was start coaching Little League involving both my boys and my girls. Then I became athletic director at St. Isidore's parish. And my life began to branch out in other areas, too. If it hadn't, if I had not started to balance my life at that time, I would have missed out on a lot of joys of fatherhood. It was a real effort for me to take the time to get involved with the kids, and I felt guilty out there on the athletic field, leaving work a little early, to play with the kids. But now, looking back, I think of the words to the Harry Chapin song, "Cat's in the Cradle." The song is about a father who just never had time to do the things his son asked him to, like play catch with a baseball. The boy kept saying, in the song, that he wanted to grow up to be just like his Dad. And he did—when he was grown, and Dad was getting old, and Dad asked the son to spend some time with him, the son was too busy.

One day when I got to the ball field—the boys were in the third or fourth grade, the youngest of the Little Leaguers—the crowd was cheering, and a man ran over to me and said, out of breath with excitement, "Mr. Riley, it was unbelievable."

"What, what?"

"Your son Rick just made an *unassisted triple play.*"

Rick had been playing second base and the bases had been

loaded, with no outs. He had caught the ball, run over and touched second base, and kept running to third base and touched it before the runner got back there, too. Afterward, I was so happy to be celebrating with my son.

I feel so fortunate that I was able to spend that time with the kids. And the gratifications of coaching led me to make other changes. I started by thinking about my net worth. I was financially successful; I had stocks and bonds—but I realized that I didn't really know what it all meant. And what good was it? What was I going to do—tuck it away in a sock and keep it hidden? Why not allow the fruits of my effort to enrich life *now*?

I looked at the things I like to do—being outdoors, physical activity, nature and the sun, being with my family, sweating—and I sold my stocks and bonds and invested instead in a ranch. My kids and I went there every weekend. I leased it out to a rancher, but we would go there every weekend.

We named it Paradise Valley Ranch. We had fun naming its features. There's a little lake, and it's now LaVerne Lake. A hill we called Rick's Ridge, and we named Nancy's Knoll, Kathy's Valley, and Bob's Brook. It all tied in with the relationships in the family. It was wonderful for us—and it was also a nice tax writeoff.

By the way, such a ranch is one of the few investments where you can actually write off money paid for the family's work efforts. What we did was to draw up an agreement that the pay that the kids earned on the ranch went toward their college education. Their pay was a writeoff I could deduct from gross income. While they were helping to enhance the value of the property, we were working together and growing closer. As I look back at how quickly they are gone—all of them have graduated from college now—I think, "I'm so glad I did that."

I call all these enjoyments "psychic income." For example, when I first bought the ranch, it did not look like the best investment. As it happened, it turned out to be a very good investment, economically. But I also got psychic income from it, and that motivated me to sit down and measure the psychic income.

How do you do that? I counted the many hours of pleasure, the increase of family closeness by 50%, and many other, related returns.

We had a couple of horses at the ranch for the girls. If I had not had those horses on the ranch, it would have cost me X dollars to duplicate their riding time at home. And just in general we were all getting so much more out of life. There were the closeness and the stress reduction, which were wonderful. I'd go up there for a weekend and then feel great the whole next week. These were really priceless benefits for a relatively small payment.

So I feel sorry for people who are so successful that they think they can't take that kind of time off. They don't see the importance of it. They get so many strokes where they are that they don't think they need to get other kinds of strokes—and more satisfying ones—elsewhere. But I had needed to get something else. I had felt like I was trapped.

My whole leisure life improved, and my fatherhood role improved. That was what was important to me. Nowadays I think many companies are more open to that kind of thing, but this was back in the Sixties. The thing is, you can't know, when you make the choice—consciously or by default—what changing your path will accomplish. For example, as a result of being involved in the direction that I took with the ranch, our twin boys graduated from the University of California at Davis in agricultural/business programs. You can see that I consider my decision to have been important. It redirected things and enhanced our lives at the same time.

I compare my life with my father's. He never invested in much of anything other than a house, and when he retired he lived with us. To the end of his days he bought his clothes by mail order. It didn't matter to him, so long as they fit and they were cheap. Our values were different. He was from the Depression era, and he could not break that outlook. When he lived with us, his interests and activities were very narrow. He had no outlets, no balance. He was a very simple man, and relatively happy in that mold. He had a no standard for comparison. But I think he would have been happier had he branched out more.

When I got married 25 years ago, my net worth was $1,600. Because of some of the techniques that I've applied in the economic area, my net worth is now close to a million dollars, with a beautiful home in California, a 200-acre ranch, a second home on a lake, and four kids put through college. Those achievements came about mostly by goal planning and by taking small, relatively conservative steps.

Initially I thought of net worth as just in dollar terms. Now I see it as much more. My worth includes my relationships, my spiritual life, my leisure activities and accomplishments, and my purpose.

No matter what your financial goals and other goals are, you can increase your worth, your quality—in all areas—by a great deal if you will use the methods I will show you.

The first step I suggest you take is to fill out the form on the next page. It is a simple one-page form. I call it an annual financial statement, indicating financial assets and liabilities.

The fixed-dollar assets are your cash, savings, and other liquid assets. Then you add your equities—home, stocks and bonds, business interests, real-estate investments, profit-sharing plans, and so on. Then you fill in any miscellaneous assets: automobile(s), furnishings and equipment, valuables (jewelry, coins, furs, precious metals, collections), any hobby or sports equipment, and other personal property of value. Totalling all these gives you your total assets.

Now figure your liabilities. Unpaid bills currently due, charge-account balances, credit-card balances, taxes due, etc., are your current liabilities. Next figure your time payments—installment-plan balances, personal loans, and any other time payments. Finally, add in the balance due on your mortgage(s) and any other loans outstanding.

Subtracting total liabilities from total assets gives your personal or family net worth.

I use this form in managing people I work with. It isn't a requirement for my job, but I give it to my employees to help them get ahead economically.

A couple of years ago I was invited to an open house by a man who'd worked for me five or six years earlier. He had left the company to start his own business, which had prospered. He

Annual Personal/Family Statement

Assets   Date _____
  Fixed dollars:
    Cash on hand   _____
    Checking accounts   _____
    Savings accounts   _____
    Life insurance
      (Total cash value)   _____
    Annuities and retire-
      ment funds   _____
    U.S. Savings Bonds   _____
              Total Fixed Dollars _____

  Equities
    Home
    Stocks/bonds, etc.   _____
    Business interests   _____
    Real estate inv'ts   _____
    Profit-sharing plans   _____
              Total Equities _____

  Miscellaneous assets:
    Automobile(s)   _____
    Household furnishings   _____
    Valuables   _____
    Hobby & sports equip.   _____
    Other personal prop.   _____
              Total Misc. Assets _____
                    Total Assets _____

Liabilities
  Current liabilities:
    Unpaid bills   _____
    Charge accounts   _____
    Credit-card accounts   _____
    Taxes due   _____
    Other   _____
              Total Current Liabilities _____

  Time payments:
    Installment balances   _____
    Personal loans   _____
    Other   _____
    Mortgage balance   _____
    Life ins. loans   _____
              Total Time Payments _____
                    Total Liabilities _____
    PERSONAL/FAMILY NET WORTH _____

was inviting me to his celebration of the success of the business, held at a mansion in Hillsborough, which he used as a combination home and work environment. Hillsborough is one of the wealthiest communities in California. His place is the ultimate in cottage industry. It sure didn't look like any business when I pulled into the circular driveway.

We stood on the patio having cocktails, talking, and he said to me, "You know, you really helped me, you really did something for me." And I thought to myself, "Oh, gee, he's going to tell me about my business techniques or one of my business philosophies." But he said it had nothing to do with that, nothing about the day-to-day business environment, but that it was my net-worth form. He said he had used it ever since I'd given it to him.

What made that simple form so valuable to him was how he had used it. I had shared with him how I used it. After you complete the form, you can start to receive the benefits too.

The first step—and the only one he used, because that is as far as I had taken the idea when I had shown him—was to set a goal for the next year.

If your net worth is $20,000, for example, set a goal for the next year that is a little higher, like $22,000 or $23,000. Put down on the form for "Goals for the Coming Year" on the next page some small steps by which you might increase your worth. Then once a month or so look at your goal. Just look at it. Don't push, just use the goal as a positive affirmation and let it have a pulling effect on your subconscious (more on this later). Doing this is kind of a form of self-induced subliminal advertising. If you look at it enough, it gets implanted in your subconscious, and pretty soon you get pulled toward the goal. Somehow you usually get there, without killing yourself.

The Hillsborough man felt that having those goals in writing, seeing the progress he was making, and getting the positive feedback that accomplishing those small steps gave him had really helped to propel him forward into the position he was now in.

So apparently there is value not only for myself but for other people in using this form. Please now look at the "Goals" form and begin filling it out.

My Goals for the Coming Year

My personal/family total net worth: _____

Modest net-worth goal to be reached by end of year: _____

Other areas where I will enhance my value:

_____

_____

_____

_____

Changes I will make to accomplish this:

_____

_____

_____

_____

Financial assets which could be converted to more life-enhancing assets:

_____

_____

_____

_____

Miscellaneous other ideas:

_____

I know it is hard for people who aren't in sales to make any dramatic increases in their income without changing jobs, but you could get an outside job, or you could do better at what you are doing and win a promotion.

Another way to improve your value is to convert your strictly financial assets to more life-enriching assets, the way I did by taking money out of stocks and bonds and putting it into a ranch. That is only one of many possible ideas. And the idea doesn't have to be one on such a grand scale. You might sell the extra family car, buy a bicycle, and invest the difference in something that doesn't depreciate the way a car does. That way you would increase your assets and also enjoy the benefits of occasionally using the bike. Harry Browne's *How I Found Freedom in an Unfree World* has a number of suggestions along these lines.

As you can see, I have expanded the financial goal-setting form to include life-enhancing values. I wanted a way of measuring and goal-setting for myself that wasn't just financial. I wanted to look at other areas of my life and aim toward enhancing my general value, using these techniques to optimize and balance my holdings. This form shows you how.

Set your financial goals. You can reach them. I met my goals every year for the past 25 years except two or three times when big emergencies drained our resources. In many years I surpassed my goals spectacularly. You can, too. Go ahead. Take that first small step now!

Chapter 5

LEISURE

Oh, how I love to run on the ridge.
As far as balance is concerned, it's my bridge.

What do you do for fun?

Do you do the same few things and sometimes wonder if you're in a rut? Do you think you don't have time to play? Do you believe you don't deserve to have fun, that play is frivolous? Do you think play has to cost a lot of money that you don't have? Do you waste a lot of leisure time and seldom have any pleasant memories to show for it?

If you said yes to any of those questions, I hope to show you that leisure time can be spent constructively and joyfully—and that it is an important part of a balanced life.

Leisure time is the time you have that isn't scheduled by someone else or by basic needs. Even after you deduct sleeping, dressing, eating, commuting, working, obligatory social activities, and time scheduled for family demands, you still have as much as 60 hours a week. Have you ever looked at it that way?

Ten years ago I was excited by my work—it was my whole life. I really didn't know what to do with myself in my free time. If I wasn't working, I was bored. I dreaded weekends, and always tried to find some work I could take home to do.

In addition, I was 40 pounds overweight, my blood pressure was climbing to 156/96, and my cholesterol level was 350 mgs.

I went to a doctor because I felt bad and he said, "Mr. Riley, you should consider starting an exercise program and changing your diet."

My dad had had carotid-artery bypass surgery, and I started to see the handwriting on the wall: I was a Type A, and a candidate for the same thing. I had a lot of stress at work, and my body was heading for a breakdown.

The day after the eye doctor told me he could tell I had too much cholesterol, I decided I was going to start running. I was scared. I put on my tennis shoes and ran around the back yard a few times. That was all I could do. It was boring and dumb and I didn't like it. I was too embarrassed to go out onto the street because I was in such bad shape. I couldn't run even half a block. I was 47 years old.

I went to a cardiologist. He examined me thoroughly and gave me a stress test. He told me that I was a good candidate for a heart attack. I ran in the back yard some more. I kept it up because I didn't want to die. Jogging at first wasn't any fun, and I wouldn't have called it leisure.

Even after I worked up to running in the streets, I could not run half a mile without having pain in my legs. They hurt so bad I would have to stop to massage them. But I kept going. I ran one block, and said to myself, "If I can run one block, then maybe next week I can run two blocks. And if I can run two blocks, I can run three." Finally one morning I ran my first mile without stopping. It took me about a month to work up to being able to run a mile continuously. When I did that, I was out on Danville Boulevard at 6:30 in the morning. I had just seen the film *Rocky,* and I jumped up and down, my hands in the air. The people driving by must have thought I was insane. But it was a great feeling, let me tell you.

I didn't realize until then how much of a jock I really am, how important athletics are to me. I had let a lot of that go when I got involved in business. You do what is expected, put your soul into your work, and eat what they sell you on television. I was just drifting along in the stream of society instead of determining my own direction.

When I was a kid, I loved sports and worshiped the

Olympians. I loved to play basketball, baseball, football, all the traditional sports. But as I mentioned earlier, I was so small that I couldn't even make the lightweight football team in high school—I was something like 4 feet 10 inches and weighed less than 100 pounds. Still I tried to compete in football and basketball.

One of the worst experiences I ever had was when I was cut from the basketball team because I couldn't successfully compete with boys who were 6'4" or more. Being cut from the team hurt me so badly I cried—and then I went over to the YMCA and started a team in their league. I ended up as high scorer of that league for that year. That experience helped to shape my life, because ever since then I've been the kind of person who says, "If you think I can't do that, then I will show you." That reaction is built into my soul now. I remember I got a little medal at the end of that basketball season, and I think that is one reason for my fascination with being competitive and winning medals now, at my age.

I am an athlete. That is me. I now accept that. When I was coaching, I was not just doing it for the kids, but for myself too. I loved to get out there and hit fly balls to the girls on the softball team. I always hoped that only nine kids would show up for my CYO basketball team practice, so I would have to play one of the positions during scrimmage.

Now I use my leisure time for actualizing the physical and social person that I am. I have gotten involved in distance running and triathlons, and in my 52nd year I finished one triathlon a week, ever single week: 52 triathlons to celebrate my 52nd year. It's an athletic world record and is listed in the 1985 *Guinness Book of Records*. My leisure life now matches who I am and what I want. As a bonus, my health is now excellent. Triathlons, which include three aerobic activities—running, biking, and swimming—are wonderful for balanced fitness. No wonder they are called the sport of the 80's.

Thus, that threat to my health took me from a very boring leisure existence to a level of accomplishment I would never have imagined. Now I have so many enjoyable things I want to do in my leisure time that it is hard to get them all done.

The interesting thing is that I didn't *have* to do any triathlons to improve my health. I got almost all the health improvement just by running five miles or 40 minutes at a time. I didn't have to break any records. I was competing because I liked doing it and because I wanted to see how far I could go.

If you want to start gaining the benefits of aerobic exercise, you don't have to do what I did. To get 90% of the benefit, all you have to do is work up to running five miles continuously, or its equivalent in your favorite sport, three times a week. This will also burn off approximately 500 calories each time!

In the first surge of my enthusiasm for endurance fitness, I put all my Type A behavior into the task. I drove myself to every limit, and strove for greater and greater heights. I wouldn't call that balance today. But I'm not doing that any more. I'm in a new phase of my life where it's not so important to me to try to win everything. I don't know if I'm just mellowing with age, or if my understanding of the importance of balance overcame my Type A tendency.

I do know that rather than training all the time to try to win these triathlons, I now aim for something else. Health is part of my value system, recognition is too, and so I'm damn happy to come in third and get the last medal. Now that I don't feel I have to win, I can, if I feel like it, party a little bit the night before.

An example comes to mind: My wife and I went to the Walnut Creek Masters Annual Swim Party a few years ago. We were celebrating the coming marriage of the swim coach. Some really fine swimmers and triathletes were there, world-class people. The top triathletes sat together at a table, and never even got out on the dance floor. I danced for an hour and a half. Maybe the difference between those triathletes and me was that they were protecting themselves. Maybe it was more important to them to win than to enjoy dancing. I was glad I was dancing. Possibly they were so totally oriented to winning that they weren't having such a good time as I was.

That event reinforced my attitude that I'd rather have balance and come in only third than not have balance. What if I got no medal at all? I'd probably be disappointed, but I'd handle it somehow. For example, I went to a triathlon in Atlanta in

1985 with a desire to win a medal, feeling that California triathletes should beat the hell out of George good ol' boys. Unfortunately, though, I was nursing a little ankle problem (my excuse), so I wasn't able to train. I came in fifth in my division. I didn't win a medal—but I did qualify for the national championships. Now, I had decided ahead of time that winning a medal would be great, but qualifying for the championships would be adequate. Not doing either of those would have meant not meeting my goal. I don't know how I would have felt if I hadn't done either. In most of these triathlons, I have placed. Once, in the Sierra Nevada Triathlon, I don't know where I placed. I was so tired afterward that just finishing was an accomplishment. I was happy to have finished because it was such a tough course.

If that Sierra Nevada event had come earlier in my fitness career, when I was more competitive, I might have been more upset. But by now I have accomplished quite a few things, so I'm willing not to spend so much time training. I achieve athletic balance by engaging in a lot of activities, too—like windsurfing and ice skating and other new things.

The social life that surrounds my fitness program also means a lot to me. For example, a few years ago I joined the Berkeley Runners. On Monday nights I would run with them up to Lake Temescal and back, and then we'd have a pizza and a beer. Those folks were different from the people I ran with on Wednesday nights, the Diablo Road Runners, in Lafayette. There we ran around the reservoir. But with both groups there was a commonality. It was very easy to talk; there was no barrier to get through with those people. And they were both lively groups.

Now my wife and I have joined the Hash House Harriers, runners who take a route determined by a unique set of rules and who are not as competitive. With them, a run is as much a social as an athletic event. I'm not sure whether there are more beer drinkers than runners in the club or the other way around; it's sort of a combination. We met recently over in Moraga at St. Mary's College and ran up into the hills for about six miles. Everything was so green—those hills were just totally verdant.

It was like what I picture New Zealand must be like. There we were, up there with the cows and soaring buzzards, running through pastures and over ridges. We ended at a pub called The Moraga Barn and danced and had a fun evening. It is a wonderful way to forget about the economic and work side of life for a while and just enjoy.

The way you use your leisure depends on you. There is no right way. You have to determine what your values are, and what makes you feel good. Be selective. Do what you really like to do.

Look at the leisure activities you now engage in. Do you participate or do you generally observe? What is your definition of leisure, anyway? I find when I ask ten people, I get ten different answers. I know that ultimate endurance triathlons are not leisure for a lot of people.

Are you a spectator at events you'd like to be participating in? Might there not be a way you could participate? Wouldn't you rather, for example, be playing a game of touch football than watching a professional game on the tube?

No two people are going to have the exact same leisure interests. But just as we tried to balance our work life by matching up our skills and our interests, we will do that in our leisure life, too.

The process is the same, no matter what you choose: You make time for yourself to enjoy an activity, and then you do it. You are going to learn to understand yourself better by evaluating how you want to spend your leisure time, and then taking small steps toward it.

My leisure activities are mostly physical. Yours may be artistic, intellectual, social, or competitive in some other way, as with cards or board games. If you like to talk and to tell stories, you might want to join the Toastmasters. Or you might want to do handwork of some kind, like carpentry or sewing, or making model airplanes. Or maybe you just want to do totally passive things. Ask yourself: Could you do a lot more than you're doing now? Attending performances, sunbathing, reading, going on guided bus tours—the opportunities are endless.

Whatever you choose, you can take it a long way. Suppose

you are interested in sailing, but have never sailed. You might start by visiting the small-boat harbor nearest you, and talking with people about your interest. That could easily lead to an invitation to help crew on a boat some Sunday afternoon. You could take a course in boat handling, which could lead to an invitation to take a trip down the coast for a week. Imagine where that could go—you could end up on a championship team of sailors doing the Transpacific. (Excuse me. I get carried away with competitive fantasies. You may not do that.)

But you get the idea. Small steps lead just as surely as large ones to distant goals. There are official and unofficial quantifications of excellence, ways of proving excellence, in virtually every area of leisure. Find out what the measurement standards are in your area of interest.

Recently I head a woman on a radio talk show ask the host how she could meet people. He told her to join a singles group. My advice would have been entirely different. I would have first suggested that she determine what her true leisure interests were, and then find opportunities to be with people who had similar interests. I think it is more important to start with an internal search to discover what your needs and desires are, and then look for what there is in society that comes closest to filling your needs and desires.

Remember what Bernie Haldane said about dependable skills. Using them leads automatically to less stress and more confidence, in leisure as well as work. When you go into a situation that calls upon your strengths, you have a much better chance of being actualized in that particular situation.

Whatever you determine you enjoy doing, there are all kinds of people doing it already. All you have to do is find them. I use a local newspaper called *City Sports* because I'm interested in athletics; it has helped me find some great people. Before, I really had few friends, and the "friends" I had were work-related acquaintances. I wasn't trying to figure out who I was and what turned me on, and then associating with people who were similar. So my weekends were boring and I was missing something important in life.

Being actualized in leisure will help to give you extra energy for other areas of your life, like work. As more leisure time becomes available to us Americans, it becomes more important for us to plan what to do with it. The use of leisure time is a growing, national problem. Many people don't know what to do with themselves when they aren't working. When I was totally oriented to work, I didn't have a handle on my free time. I felt uncomfortable on the weekends; I just didn't feel right. I had never thought about having some goals in the leisure area, or utilizing the techniques in leisure that had helped me in my work life.

This book gives you a technique for discovering what path to a quality leisure life you want to take. It applies for everyone. There are 114 items on the Leisure Preferences list on the next pages. And if that isn't enough—if you can't find things you think should be there—feel free to add them.

As before, go through the list first rating your enjoyment of each activity on the 1-to-10 scale below. When you are through, go back and rate how often you actually do each thing. When you have completed that, go back and calculate your variances again, plus or minus.

In the next column, list the actions you want to take concerning those items with a large variance. Write down the goal you'd like to aim for: "master waterskiing," or "be Dallas bridge champion," or "make a 10 x 14 rug." Underneath the goal, list the first two steps you will take toward that goal. Whatever goal you have is fine. Just write it down.

And don't forget that others are already doing the same things for fun, and they will be interesting to you because they have something in common with you. Find them. The first place to look may be as close as your corner newsstand, where you will discover periodicals covering many leisure interests. There are magazines and newspapers for most of the things on the Leisure Preferences list. You can use the specialized periodicals to find out where things are happening. You can join the groups, go to the classes, or visit the places that are of interest to you.

By the way, this is also an excellent way to develop relationships, because as you further yourself and your personal growth, you are doing it with people like yourself. That way, relationships develop more naturally.

———————— ♣ ————————

Benefits of True Fitness From Aerobic Activity

Life-saving
Life-improving
Life-lengthening
Feels good
Replaces drugs
Better appearance
Reduces weight
Brain-stimulating
Reduces colds
Reduces heart rate
Reduces cholesterol
Reduces blood pressure
Attracts opposite sex
Feel younger
Stronger body
Handle stress better
Improves mental toughness
Fun
Improves productivity
Helps eliminate smoking
Helps eliminate bad foods
Helps eliminate drinking
Helps hypertension
Helps herpes
Helps depression
Helps mental illness
Helps prevent heart problems
Improves competitiveness
Role model for others
Gets you close to nature

Reduces appetite
Keeps you more relevant
Strengthens lungs
Base of strength for other sports
Sense of accomplishment
Promotes self-sufficiency
Increases self-worth
Clears complexion
Improves sleep
Improves circulation
Can do when old or young
Allows right-brain activity
Noble way to meet opposite sex
Strengthens bones
Spiritual at times
Lowers insurance rates
Improves bowels
Can handle weather extremes
   better
Helps self-discipline
Teaches importance of pacing
   yourself
Builds willpower
Helps you learn how to play
Helps bring inner peace
Improves relaxation
Improves dancing
Improves endurance
Makes you happy

Rating Scale

Interest

1 Absolutely none.
2 Haven't thought about it.
3 Would be happy never to do it.
4 Occasionally interested.
5 Average interest.
6 More than average interest.
7 Gladly include it.
8 Take real pleasure in it.
9 Actively look for opportunities to do it.
10 Total.

Involvement

1 Very rarely or never.
2 Very seldom.
3 Occasionally.
4 Once or twice a month.
5 Average frequency.
6 Fairly often.
7 With regularity.
8 Once a week or more.
9 Several times a week.
10 Every day or more.

This scale is just a guide. Adapt it to your own needs.

Leisure Preferences*

Activity	Enjoyment (+)	Frequency (−)	Variance (+/−)	Action
Sightseeing				
Playing games of chance				
Seeing movies				
Flower arranging				
Weaving, needlework				
Martial arts				
Human potential groups				
Jewelry making				
Bowling				
Acting, dramatics				
Bus./prof. organizations				
Attending conferences, conventions				
Reading newspapers				
Reading books				
Playing computer games				
Meditating				
Watching sporting events				
Watching TV				
Reading magazines				
Library browsing				
Garden club meetings				

*Adapted from FREE TIME, by Jan Gault, John Wiley & Sons, Inc., copyright 1983.

Activity	Enjoyment (+)	Frequency (−)	Variance (+/−)	Action
Conservation/ecology organizations				
Religious organizations				
Playing the stock market				
Answering "relationship" ads				
Museum visiting				
Social drinking				
Computer programming				
Letter writing				
Bird watching				
Using hallucinogenics				
Gossiping				
Volleyball				
Bicycling				
Cooking/baking				
Hunting				
Painting/drawing				
Football				
Snorkling or scuba diving				
Partying with friends				
Basketball				
Chess				
Flying an airplane or glider				
Window shopping				

Activity	Enjoyment (+)	Frequency (−)	Variance (+/−)	Action
Writing fiction or nonfiction				
Backgammon or other board games				
Motorcycling				
Horseback riding				
Visiting friends				
Hiking				
Fishing				
Golf				
Watching dance performances				
Model building				
Walking				
Tennis				
Singing—performance or social				
Making ceramics/ pottery				
Aerobics				
Mechanical building or repairing				
Table tennis				
Attending wrestling/ boxing events				
Sailing				
Canoeing/rafting/ kayaking				
Motor boating				
Gambling				
Electronics				
Gymnastics				

Leisure

Activity	Enjoyment (+)	Frequency (−)	Variance (+/−)	Action
Attending large social events (benefits, balls, etc.)				
Attending small social events (small dinner parties, etc.)				
Listening to records or tapes				
Sewing				
Swimming				
Carpentry				
Driving for pleasure				
Sunbathing, going to beach				
Auto repairing				
Leatherworking or other crafts				
Surfing—body, board or wind				
Auto racing				
Listening to radio				
Weight lifting, bodybuilding				
Camping, backpacking				
Attending plays				
Knitting/crocheting				
Reading aloud—plays or poetry				
Dining out				
Water skiing				
Travel—long distance				
Attending lectures				

Activity	Enjoyment (+)	Frequency (−)	Variance (+/−)	Action
Social clubs or organizations				
Playing musical instrument				
Going to nightclubs				
Card games				
Gardening				
Jogging, running				
Taking college courses				
Metalworking				
Arguing				
Lovemaking				
Playing squash/hand-ball/racquetball				
Playing billiards/pool				
Brainstorming ideas				
Puzzle solving				
Attending musical concerts				
Visiting art galleries				
Sitting and thinking				
Telephone visiting				
Skiing—downhill or crosscountry				
Parlor games				
Making plans				
Learning about subjects of interest				
Meeting new people				
Other:				

Chapter 6

RELATIONSHIPS

Will I ever really get to know thee?
Perhaps only when I solve the mystery of me.

When was the last time you created a new relationship? How much do you put into the ones you already have? If you suspect you could be getting more from the relationships in your life—and want more—this chapter is for you.

Although there are two distinct kinds of intimates in all of our lives—family and friends—the principles involved in creating and maintaining rich and rewarding relationships with them are the same. Essentially, the difference is only a matter of how we got them. Parents, siblings, children, and more distant relatives are given to us by birth. Friends, including spouses, are chosen. What we want from all these people—and what we must be prepared to give in return—is a commitment to care. We make a mutual agreement to take each other's interests to heart, and this isn't any less true just because we don't say so out loud.

Someone once said that home is the place where, when you go there, they have to take you in. In that sense, our families are glued to us more tightly than anyone else is. But in these days of unprecedented numbers of broken families, when all the old rules have been thrown up for questioning and not yet replaced by new ones, it makes sense for us all to cement relations with people outside our family circles also.

On the other hand, some people learn the value of family

relationships very late in life, and come full circle. That's what happened to me.

When I got into running I became absolutely a new person. I think I even changed chemically. I was more in control of myself. But my change wasn't all to the good. When you change like that, it affects people around you, a lot. Up to that time, I was what I would call dishonest. I had two lives: I had my family, and I also had a totally different sex life.

Part of the problem was the rhythm method. We were Roman Catholic, and my wife didn't feel comfortable using contraceptives. We were both spending a lot of time on the kids, but we weren't really spending time alone together. We had grown out of touch. Frankly, I'm not sure we had ever been in touch. We just had our roles, and we played them well. Or at least I played my father role well once each child started being able to bounce a ball. That's when I really started to take an interest. When they could play sports, I could identify with them on a physical level. But while we were spending lots of family time together, my wife and I were not really relating together. I had a secret outside life. My life was, honestly, a nonquality life.

In addition, I realized that I didn't really have any friends. All my relationships were roles. I was husband, father, sales executive, parish coach, sexual fantasizer. Then I decided that I wanted to have quality relationships, and more honesty, in my life. So I started to look for some deeper relationships, and I started with women.

I think I prefer the company of women because, starting in the Fifties, everyone I worked with was a man. I have a picture of my class in business school: seven rows of men with white shirts, dark suits, and ties, fifteen men to a row. Now when I look at that picture or think about it, I go Argghh!

I was always surrounded by men. I called on male purchasing agents and male managers. That was all there were, then. I was glad to get away from that situation to what we have today. It is so much more natural now. I enjoy business much more now that there are women in responsible positions. Before, it was ridiculous.

That was why, when I went looking for honest relationships, I made friends with women. I didn't even want to talk to men!

I had already tried to make my relationship with my wife work. We had even gone to a marriage encounter weekend, but it didn't bring us any closer. I was spending less time at home, and our relationship became boring and routine. I knew how it had happened—we had got married and had had premature twin boys before we even had a chance to get to know each other. We had had four kids in three years, and the house was full of kids all the time. But knowing how it had happened didn't make it any more desirable.

I was meeting other women in the running clubs, which made the split between home and everything else even more extreme. I was feeling better physically, and looking better, and I had more confidence. And there were lots of opportunities to get to know other women in the running scene.

Finally, my wife forced the issue. She called a family meeting, and she told us all, "Dad's just drifting away. Me, too." She wanted the family to know that we were having problems. She suggested that because I was spending very little time at home anyway, perhaps we should separate and I should move out. My wife envisioned that I would live by myself—but that wasn't the way it happened.

I had decided I needed a friend, someone who had the same lifestyle I had. I wanted a playmate, a lover, and a companion. The big reason I had not left earlier was that the economic side of my life was so important to me. I knew that if I left, I would also hurt my financial position, and perhaps it was my financial position I was trying to hold onto, rather than the relationship. Of course, the kids were important to me, but I had finally decided during a run on the ridge the very morning of our family meeting that the financial motivation was just not that important. As soon as I had made that decision, I felt free.

Once I had made that decision, everything else fell into place. I thought my wife's decision was just part of the cosmic plan. I knew that from then on, I was going to determine what kind of life I led and what kind of relationships I developed.

Even though it meant I would miss reaching the economic goal I had set myself, that was all right. It just meant changing the goal. The pain of the marriage was greater than my desire to reach the economic goal. After the separation took place, she and I both had a chance to re-evaluate our situations, to reassess our importance to each other.

I called a lady I had been running with—she had an extra bedroom—and asked her if she would mind if I moved in. She said no, she wouldn't mind, so I went that same day. I didn't know what my wife would think about that, but so far as I was concerned, our marriage was dead. I was gone and I wasn't coming back. I thought that was what she wanted.

The kids were interested in their own friends, and three were away at college. When my wife would call me, I wouldn't even want to talk to her, but I did. And I would go home to visit my daughter. But I was in an ecstatic state living in that woman's house. It was exactly ten kilometers from work, and I ran to work. It was almost as if I had designed it that way—selected my lady friend based on the distance I could run! It was 10k each way and I could change clothes at the Athletic Club, two blocks from the office. It was perfect.

My wife was very depressed. It was a real low point for her. She had been playing a role, too. But now the kids were grown and they were telling her, "We don't need you so much. You don't have to hang over us all the time." Just when she could have started devoting more time to me, I was gone. Her life was really shaken.

One day when I was visiting my daughter, my wife said she was feeling very low. I did not want to get back together at the time, but on the other hand I wanted to try to help her. I cared what happened to her. So I said that when I got depressed, I went out and ran, and that somehow helped to make me feel better. I didn't expect her to take my advice. I had never seen her run a day in her life except when she took off her shoe to run across the family room to whack one of the kids if they misbehaved.

Lo and behold, she went out and bought some running shoes and started puffing around the back yard, the way I had done.

Pretty soon she was running out on the roads. She began to get more vitality and started to look a lot better in my eyes. When I was home visiting, she would even do some runs with me. And we went to a race or two together. We started to go to counseling, where we realized we had some bad communication problems. The counselor helped us begin to understand each other a lot better.

The counseling seemed to be having a positive effect, and my other relationship wasn't working out that well. The lady I was living with wanted to get married. So she went back together with a man she'd known before, and I moved home. The counseling helped more and more, and my wife and I kept running together and going to running events.

A big event for me was the Senior Olympics. They're for people over 30. They divide the competitions up by age class: 30 to 40, 40 to 50, and so on. I wanted to win a medal in the 50+ age 10,000-meter race. That was one of my dreams. I had been in training for a long time. My wife and I were getting closer and closer, so I said to her, "I'm going down for the Senior Olympics in Los Angeles. Come on along." She said okay.

The morning of the event I signed up for the race, and noticed that they also had a 10,000-meter race for women in her age class. So I suggested she sign up.

"No, I don't want to," she said.

I signed her up anyway. She didn't want to do it, but she decided to try. Now, I was the one who had dreamed and trained for this, who yearned to win a medal. I came in 7th in my race, and my wife won the *gold medal* in hers! We hugged at the end of her race. She knew I was disappointed in my race, and with careful sensitivity she told me that my coaching had helped her to win. Her medal hangs on our mantelpiece today.

Because I was receiving so many benefits from running, I had wanted a relationship with somebody who was into the running world, maybe even someone who had some credibility in that world. I had wanted someone I could really talk to about what was important to me, somebody I could play with, somebody I could hang out with. I had wanted to be the real me, no roles, nothing, just open and true. Then suddenly, somehow, this lady, this wife of mine, had transformed herself and now was the person I had wanted. I don't know whether it's in my eyes or her eyes or what, but it happened, and it's incredible.

She has changed considerably, it seems to me. She feels that I have too. We both see the other in a new light. And we both find in each other something more of what we wanted and couldn't give each other before. This, at any rate, is the way I see it, and she says the same thing has happened in her perception. So we both got more of what we wanted, and didn't have to sever the relationship. That is great.

Our relationship has grown much deeper, so I no longer have much inclination to reach out to other relationships. But that is a bit scary, because if something happened to the relationship with my wife, I've put all my eggs in one basket and I'd be devastated. She means more to me now than she ever did before. I've never really had a truly deep relationship like the one we have now. It's like running a marathon the first time: gratifying and rewarding on so many levels. And sometimes painful, too. My wife is experiencing the same profound feelings.

She's more open now, too. I have a feeling that I'm helping her to be happier, which is a great feeling. I never thought about that much before. We were just sort of "doing" life in a partnership. Now I can feel that because of our association she is happier. I can see it in photographs. Our kids see it, too. In the past year her expression has been fuller, more lively. She's definitely in a renaissance of her own. She's in a passage from the period where she wasn't needed as a mother any more to a period of creating a new life for herself. I'm proud to be doing it with her.

In the course of hiring for various companies I've worked for, I've talked with a lot of people, and one of the questions I ask is, "What do you consider the greatest success in your life, and what was your biggest failure?" The successes varied a lot, but one of the failure answers came up again and again: "My divorce." The failure was the marriage not working.

I'm just lucky that I have this lady who is now the image of what I wanted to go on to, yet I still have the past and I still have the family. We had three kids graduate from college last year, and one got married. It was a big year for our family. We had several celebrations in honor of those events, and my wife and I probably had more fun than the children.

Those events were much more important than triathlons and medals, by far. We've managed to reach the point with the kids where it's just easy being around one another. There's no stress or strain, nobody bugging anybody; we all accept one another. This is a situation everybody wants but few people get.

Perhaps one of the determining factors in our success as a family was my decision not to move every two years, continuing up the ladder of business success. Fortunately, the moment that I realized that there were other things in life besides business was exactly the moment that the kids reached the stage where I could really identify with them. So I was able to spend time with them, time I wouldn't have had if I'd been still totally devoting myself to work.

We are blessed with some really good kids. I think we both contributed to that, my wife to the greater extent because she was home with them much more. The roles of father and mother are a wonderful part of the completion of life.

Many people who are not really happy never go on to the next possible stage of life. They live in worn-out, lukewarm, nonactualizing relationships because they let society, to a great degree, make choices for them. They hang on to marriages because that is what society expects of them. Women, especially, used to hang on because they were financially dependent. Nowadays women are more likely to hang on from habit or emotional dependency. To suffer builds character, they tell themselves.

Such people socialize with other people from work, or with the parents of their children's friends. I've found that to open one door more fully, you often have to close another completely. It's the same in relationships. If we hang on to old relationships, out of habit or comfort, we can't enter into new ones. I came to the point where I saw the important thing is *being:* Day-to-day-living is more important than trying to stay in old relationships one has outgrown—nonquality relationships. I didn't used to think that about relationships. For two or three years I was afraid to go through new doors. It can be very scary, but often it is what we have to do in order to have quality in our lives. It's a matter of progressing through our life stages, moving on. In the past my goals were concerned mainly with work. I didn't realize you could have as much excitement reaching for and achieving relationship goals. Building more quality in family or friend relationships can give one a great return on the emotional investment.

One of the things I did when I was studying the subject of relationships—both in my life and in books and journals, as a research subject—was to take some interesting tests that I found at the University of California-Berkeley Psychological Testing Library. I found and took a pair-attraction test, a caring-relationship test, and a personal-profile test. They were excellent self-introspection tools. The personal-profile test showed me that I was a goal-oriented person, and gave me some good information about who it would be good for me to have around in order to balance my strengths and my weaknesses. What struck me was that my wife fit the picture of that balancing force. She is very different from me, and has many of the qualities I lack.

We'd talked, over the years, about how different we are from each other. I'm a go-get'em, charge, impatient, hyper, Type A person—very outgoing. LaVerne is much more a calming influence, a very level-headed and conservative person. Sometimes we wonder how we got together. But the test showed me that she was really the kind of person I need for me to survive. She complements me, and I complement her.

If I had a woman like myself, it might be fun, briefly, but I'm afraid we'd kill each other after a short time.

I took the personal-profile test home and showed it to my wife. It helped us to understand the how and the why of our relationship. It really made us understand each other and our marriage better. I think that going through a matching up of personal values and strengths and weaknesses is very helpful to strengthen key relationships.

Now I do have other relationships, too. Friends. I still have more female friends than male. I still haven't gotten over the overkill in men in the earlier part of my life. Maybe I'm over-reacting to my own history. Still I do have a number of men friends.

Until recently, most American men and women left their old friendships at the altar when they married. To do that leaves one bereft, in a way. There is nothing promiscuous about loving more than one person in this world, caring about and supporting emotionally as many people as we can handle. But marriage in the past tended to diminish the importance of other friends.

Single people, by default, are more highly motivated to have good friendships. That's where they get their emotional goodies. Hopefully, they are willing to pay the price of real friends: hard work. You must invest time and a lot of yourself, your attention, in friends.

There are as many levels of depth and permutations of arrangement possible with friendships as there are with marriage. Friendships broken by disappointment or disloyalty or lack of caring are just as unlikely to be renewed as broken marriages.

An important characteristic of a quality relationship is duration. How long has it been going on? Another characteristic is that the parties see one another with some regularity. And the relationships must withstand some tests, like financial adversity or illness. Things need to happen between us so we can really get to know each other. When you have been in a relationship for 25 years, and suffered through the heartaches and joys together, you have a sense of having built something together that was not easy, and pride in having built it. Sometimes it helps just to stand back and admire that emotional cathedral.

The Relationship Balance Sheet is a tool for analyzing your relationships. It will help you quantify and qualify the people in your life. As with the previous self-analyses, it is very important that you approach this one with great honesty, openness, and vulnerability. You can do this privately in your home, with no one peering over your shoulder. If many of the relationships you're going to be looking at are in your home, and you don't have a private place to do it, get away from the house by yourself.

This self-analysis gives you the variance, if any, between your honest appreciation of each of your relationships and how much time you actually spend on them. You can easily see whom you want to spend more time with—and whom less.

The Relationship Balance Sheet is like the ones you have already filled out, but shorter. You simply write in the names of the people closest to you, the people who make up your "social life." After you've written the names, go to the top of the next column and write in a score of 1 to 10, indicating how you honestly feel about that person. Rate each person not on any objective scale, but on how much you really think of them as a friend for you. What is your true level of personal appreciation for each of the names on your list? Take your time.

Then go back to the next column and on the same 1-to-10 scale choose a number that represents how frequently you see the person. Rarely would be a 1, daily communication a 10.

Now look at the variances. If there is a variance of more than 3 for any person, you may want to change how you relate to that person. For each of the names with a large variance, write in the Action column what steps you want to take.

If you see a person with a frequency of 8, but your honest appreciation is only a 3, you could think of ways to cut down. You could, for example, stop having Sunday dinner and riding in a carpool with that person. If a big minus variance exists with a family member, obviously there is a problem. Instead of just living with the problem, take some action. Perhaps a frank discussion will help. Family counseling professionals are available to help improve poor or faltering relationships. It's amazing how counseling can help.

You might also want to add the names of people you rarely see, and don't know well, but want to get to know. What will you do to develop the relationship? You can even decide to meet new people altogether, and add a mysterious X to the list. Think of steps you can take to find a new friend. One place to start would be among your new leisure-activity acquaintances.

Relationship Rating Scale

Enjoyment

1 Hate being with them.
2 Avoid them actively.
3 Would be happy never to be with them.
4 Rarely pleasurable.
5 Average.
6 Really don't mind them at all.
7 Gladly include them.
8 Take real pleasure in being with them.
9 Actively look for opportunities to be with them.
10 Wonderful. Love being with them.

Frequency

1 Very rarely or never.
2 Very seldom.
3 Occasionally.
4 Once a month or two.
5 Average frequency.
6 Fairly often.
7 With regularity.
8 Once a week or more.
9 Several times a week.
10 Every day or more.

This scale is just a guide. Adapt it to your own needs.

Relationship Balance Sheet

Name of person (One to a line)	Honest Appre-ciation (+)	Frequency (−)	Variance (+/−)	Action

Chapter 7

SPIRITUALITY

The nature of God appears to me
In sun and sky and Sierra tree.

Spirituality can be a hard idea to grasp. If you have a comfortable fit with some religious denomination and you're happy with it, then you may not have any further interest in this chapter. Just go on to the next. But if you have experienced a yearning to be connected with something larger than yourself, your family, or other immediate environment, and if you have always suspected that there was something you could do that would allow you to feel a part of that larger something, then read on.

Some definitions are called for here. By "spirituality," I mean a sense of essential connection with the universe. That may come to you through any of a wide variety of ways: organized religion, altered states of consciousness, pagan rituals, music, meditation, massage—or even (here comes the plug) aerobic endurance activities. And these are only a few of the limitless possibilities.

In our organized society, organized religion is for most people the method of choice for their spiritual life. It has stood the test of tens of centuries, and people continue to find daily personal meaning in its practices. By definition, a religion is a set of codified beliefs and practices, usually built upon the teachings of one particularly spiritually evolved person.

Spirituality is in some ways larger than any one religion, and in some ways smaller. One can have a connection with the universe without any organized ceremony or belief system, but a religion supplies a structure and rules for living that many people seem to need.

I was a conventional churchgoer for most of my life. Churchgoing fit well the life we lived, and was a good family experience. It was structured with many family kinds of activities and that was good, but I never really got deeply involved in my organized religion until a few years ago.

One hot summer day when I was sitting in church, I saw the little girl in front of me faint. I lifted her up and carried her outside, over to the door of the rectory. Monsignor Bensen came to the door and ushered us in, and I put the girl on his couch. While we awaited her parents, we talked, he and I, and he mentioned that he was looking for people to be active in the parish.

A week later he called me and asked if I would become involved in the education for the grade schools. I was teaching at the time, so I agreed, if reluctantly. He made me president of the board that oversaw the youth program for about a thousand kids. But it was really just a figurehead position, and as soon as the athletic directorship for the CYO program opened up, I quickly transferred to that. I felt much more at home doing that kind of thing, and eventually I coached athletics for five years.

During that time I got to know Monsignor Bensen quite well. He was a very gentle, spiritual man and a very loving man. He was my first real spiritual role model. He let me see that you could accomplish things without having to jump up and down and yell and holler. My tendency had always been to be hyper, to get all excited, and then not to accomplish much in the end. He was just the opposite, and I found myself really wanting to do things for him. I did more in a very short period of time for that church than I had done in my whole life for religious organizations, and he was the motivating force for all that. We never did talk much about religion.

At the time, I was working in San Francisco. A combina-

tion of boredom at work and a lack of sense of purpose drove me
to look for something more than what was in my life then. At
lunchtime, I usually went out of the building and did something
different, seeking out interesting and stimulating ways to spend
the time. One day I found a Paulist Center on Grant Avenue in
San Francisco, behind Old St. Mary's Church. It had a spiritual
library with books and audio and video tapes.

One noontime I found there a video series narrated by Ron
Eyre of the British Broadcasting Company. Called "The Long
Search," it was a twelve part series devoted to investigating
twelve different religions to discover what qualities they had
which had given them such staying power. Eyre had spent a
year traveling the world, inquiring nonjudgmentally about the
key elements and unique essences of these religions. He talked
to both clergy and lay people, rich and poor, digging down to
find the meaning that their religion held for them.

For several weeks that was what I'd do with my lunch hour:
take a brown bag over to the Paulist library and put on one of the
videotapes. I was fascinated. I went in with the approach of a
student, and found myself doing my own analysis of the different religions and looking at my own spiritual values and what
in these religions appealed to me. It seemed that there must be
some real significance to these religions that made them last,
and I wanted to discover what gave them their longevity. Then I
wanted to incorporate what I had learned into my own life. I
thought it would help me balance myself, and would increase
the quality of my life. I had no idea I was taking only the first
steps in a long odyssey.

You know by now that I really like to quantify things. I'm
always doing what I call gut statistics. For example, as I drive to
work, I'll look down other streets and try to estimate the fastest
route. It is part of my nature and my approach to life. So at the
library I made notes, evaluating each of the religions. For each
one, certain key characteristics were identified by the narrator
of the series, so I could make solid comparisons. Those beliefs,
practices, and values that appealed to me I wrote down. At the
end of the series of twelve religions, I had 37 key characteristics that I really liked.

And I thought to myself, "If those points are keystones of these religions that have lasted for thousands of years, and I like them, then I ought to try to put more of them into my life."

I looked at the Roman Catholic Mass. There were certain parts that I liked, and other parts that I didn't really understand and couldn't identify with. So I decided to develop, from what I had learned from "The Long Search," a list of things I liked, and then I designed my own Mass. I designed it in order to actualize the spiritual experience that I wanted.

If this idea frightens or offends you, go on to the next chapter because what I am describing is just one person's search for a higher level of spiritual involvement and meaning.

I was also traveling for my company in those days, and I wanted some spiritual exercise I could use when I was alone on a weekend in a strange city. It was an exciting thought, one I'd never had before. What I developed for myself went onto a card I carried with me, and it went something like this:

First I would spend time relaxing and getting into an accepting, receptive state, with my eyes closed in a quiet setting. Then I gave thanks for recent good things and reviewed in my mind what had happened during the past week. I took time to think about the people I was involved with, and the situations. I spent time thinking about the coming week, planning to carry out my activities on a more spiritual plane than in earlier times, and taking a thankful attitude toward what was to come. It was a small ceremony of thankfulness, thoughtfulness, and meditation. I found real value in it, and I still do it today, in a modified form. It is my unique way of getting in touch with my spiritual dimensions, and it is personally gratifying.

I've found that incorporating these spiritual ideas into the rest of my life has elevated it, and brought more quality into all the other areas. It affects my work, my relationships, my sense of purpose, and even my leisure, in that I have more spiritual moments whatever I'm doing.

I can't begin to tell you all the ways that my life has been enriched by adapting some spiritual practices to my own needs. Perhaps you can imagine how it could improve my relationships and my work, but let me tell you about what it does for my running.

You know that the left brain has more logical capability, whereas the right brain does more of the artistic, or feeling, kinds of things. In Western society in general—and in American men in particular—the mental focus is very left-brain oriented. Long-distance running pulls the mind over to the right side.

For example, on a Sunday morning in Spring, I will get up and go for a run on the ridge in the Las Trampas hills behind my house. The first mile and a half is uphill, and I'm really sweating. My training has provided me with the physical means to do it easily, and at the beginning of the run I am goal-oriented and busy thinking about conventional things. But near the top of the mountain I move into another mode: I stop looking at the linear pattern of the run, and instead become more than a runner; in some way I am the running. And I perceive the world around me in a kind of oneness. Time ceases to have meaning, and I don't think about my body. I get above the plain, with the ridge behind me, and I can see over the valley toward Mt. Diablo. It may be foggy in the valley, but I can see the sun rising over the fog, and the mountain poking above the layer of white. It is breathtaking.

Then I wonder, why am I the only person on the ridge? Why don't other people realize the beauty that is here? And then a voice comes in from the left brain and reminds me that if they did, it would be crowded here, and much less glorious.

I feel at one with the hills, the fog, the cows, and the sun. I am part of the greater whole, and it is good. I can really "feel." Sometimes the tears flow, just from the beauty and wonder of it.

I've had many mystical experiences in running marathons. In the last part—probably the last six miles—all logic is gone and I'm just experiencing the indescribable event.

During my second marathon, at Sacramento, my foot began to hurt badly at about 23 miles. I slowed to a walk. Suddenly it seemed like there was a fog around me, even though it was an otherwise clear day. A person loped past me and went about half a block ahead. Then he stopped, turned around, and made a beckoning wave toward me. It was eerie. I could see this man with a beard through the fog, and he was waving a come-with-me gesture.

I had a sudden thought that Jesus was asking me to go with him, but rejected the idea. The man was still beckoning to me. I looked behind me, thinking he must have a friend coming along, because I knew I didn't know him. But no one else was there. He was still waving, so I started running again. My foot didn't hurt much any more. I ran up abreast of him and we ran along together for a while.

I finally said, "Why did you turn around and wave at me?"

"I just felt like you needed help," he said, "and I wanted to help you."

I ran the rest of the way. When I arrived at the finish, I wanted to thank him, but he was nowhere in sight!

It is an incredible feeling when the sharing part of the experience—the brotherhood and sisterhood of marathoners—comes out like that. Your barriers collapse and you feel an irrevocable kinship. You can't go back to feeling isolated, ever again.

When I think back and realize how I never used to appreciate the world around me—my work was everything—I see how far I've come.

I'm still on my spiritual quest, and expect always to be. The areas of possible development really are infinite. When I find new answers and compare them to the old ones, they all seem to fit. As Aldous Huxley said once, when asked how he could keep accepting new spiritual ideas, one after another:

"They are all right."

The thing I remember most from my study of Buddhism was an interview the BBC series narrator had with a monk. After traveling hundreds of miles to a secluded monastery in the Himalayas to find him, he asked this meditative man, "What is the purpose of life? What is our reason for being here? What should we think of as important?"

The monk, a quiet, frail individual, paused for a while and then replied quietly, "I can't answer that. You have to. And when you do, you must be honest with yourself."

How many of us really understand and accept ourselves and feel good about who we are, regardless of what society thinks we ought to be? The truth is that it is easier in the short run not to bother with any of this. But if we haven't thought about who we really are and what we really believe, then when a crisis hits our lives, we don't have the resources to cope. I guess it is human nature to wait to do something until we absolutely have to. I look back on those circles of cholesterol in my eyes and shake my head in wonder. I say to myself, look how far I had to go in the wrong direction before I was willing to change. And I know most people are like I was.

Each of us has a unique spiritual need. Perhaps that becomes more obvious as we mature. Or perhaps the need grows with age, as it did for me. As I moved through my passages I had to have more to my spiritual life.

The next self-analysis is the Spiritual Experience Preference form. I've included all 37 of the qualities I liked which I found in the BBC series. As before, I ask you to rate your preferences on a scale of 1 to 10. Then go back and rate your frequency of experiencing each of those qualities. As before, write in the variances.

There could be more qualities on your list. Since we all see things entirely differently in this self-analysis, you may think of other forms of worship, values, or practices that mean a lot to you. Add them to the list. The idea is to create your own "religion," one that offers the spiritual environment you need and has the most possible meaning for you.

My ideal religion would have to have sexual equality. It seemed that in those religions I studied, not one had true equality. They all seemed to be very much male-dominated. For example, my sons were altar boys in church, like other sons. When my daughters were that age, I would have liked them to be altar girls, but nobody ever heard of that. I would have been willing to make an issue of it, but my daughters never showed any interest. So I just let it go.

Now I sometimes attend a nearby church. It has a woman pastor, Carol Ruth Knox. I really like her. The church is a very ecumenical environment, combining East and West, and the ceremony is more of an internal experience for me. That makes it more meaningful.

When you have finished calculating variances on the

Spiritual Experience Preference form, notice which ones have a significant variance and think about what action you want to take concerning them. Small steps, remember—one doesn't create an entire religion overnight.

But you might also want to think about a way you could formalize some of your spiritual experience preferences. Could you create a ritual or ceremony around them? Is that something you'd like to do?

Applying these techniques will make your spiritual life much richer and fuller.

Spiritual Rating Scale

Interest

1 Absolutely none.
2 Haven't thought about it.
3 Can certainly do without it.
4 Occasionally interested.
5 Average interest.
6 More than average interest.
7 Like it.
8 Take real pleasure in it.
9 Actively seek it.
10 Total.

Involvement

1 Very rarely or never.
2 Very seldom.
3 Occasionally.
4 Once or twice a month.
5 Average frequency.
6 Fairly often.
7 With regularity.
8 Once a week or more.
9 Several times a week.
10 Every day or more.

This scale is just a guide. Adapt it to your own needs.

Spiritual Experience Preference

Quality (Forms of worship, values, and practices)	Preference (+)	Frequency (−)	Variance (+/−)	Action
Nature				
Sun				
Water				
Trees				
Stones				
Holistic concepts				
Nutrition				
Wellness principles				
Music/dance				
Silence				
Prayer				
Calm/deliberation				
Confession				
Relaxation				
Meditation				
Giving				
Helping				
Golden Rule				
Compassion				
Respect for elders				
Sense of oneness				
Growing nearer to God				
Self-improvement				
Knowing thy self				
Mystery				
Family togetherness				

Quality (Forms of worship, values, and practices)	Preference (+)	Frequency (−)	Variance (+/−)	Action
Warmth of home fire				
Parents teaching child				
Sharing				
Holy places				
Holy times				
Holy persons				
Female/male equality				
Pilgrimage				
Ritual experience				
Rebirth				
Dreams				
Other				

Chapter 8

PURPOSE

Let me be and do what I love best
Only when it's over will I truly rest.

Why do you live? What is the purpose of your life? What motivates you to get out of bed in the morning? Is there meaning to your actions?

If you have thought about these questions, and then dismissed finding any answers as beyond your abilities, consider: If you don't have—or aren't working toward—your own goals, you can bet you're part of someone else's.

Right?

Think about *that*.

This chapter will help you realize what *your* purposes are, and enable you to take *small steps* to achieve them.

I've found in my seminars that many people don't know what their purposes are because their purposes are unconscious. Other people really don't have any.

One day about eight years ago when I was hiking up a hill at Lake Comanche, California, a thought hit me out of nowhere: "I wonder how much more time I've got." That's when I started to think seriously about purpose. Up to that time I really had no conscious idea of purpose. I had never thought about it. Unconsciously, my purpose was my work.

After the thought struck me, I went to a seminar given by Dr. Charles Garfield on achieving peak performance. One of the things he talked about was a study made of people who were literally on their deathbeds. They were asked to reflect on their lives. "What was important?" they were asked. "What did you do, and what happened to you that was really meaningful?" Two areas were consistently mentioned by most people in the study: the relationships they had with the people close to them, and their purpose in life. Their sense of purpose, the thing that they felt gave their life meaning, didn't necessarily have anything to do with their work.

If the question of purpose isn't faced earlier, most people have to deal with it when they retire. When your work life ends, you can no longer avoid the need to have something else meaningful in life to motivate you to go on living. Most people who have no great purpose die within a few years of retirement; they simply don't have anything to keep them going.

So it's a good idea to think about purposes now. What do you want to have accomplished before you die? How do you want people to remember you? What do you want to be able to say you stood for?

To put it most succinctly, what would you like your epitaph to say? Take a few minutes and write it down here.

Gail Sheehy, the author of *Passages,* spent three years collecting 60,000 questionnaires to learn the ten keystones of well-being from the people she called Pathfinders. She said the one constant that was most important in the lives of people who enjoyed high well-being was a devotion to some cause or purpose beyond themselves.

For many, their work was their purpose, and to find meaning in one's life's work can certainly be gratifying. But Sheehy believes that it is getting much harder in America today to find meaningful work, work that is worth dedicating oneself to, than it used to be. She thinks this change is responsible for the widespread change of values from the work ethic to some other value. In many cases, the American business model treats people like machines rather than important keystones of the business. The Japanese have done an excellent job of making their workers important, and their productivity proves it.

Americans who don't find satisfaction in work look for

other things to live for. You don't have to be one of Sheehy's "Pathfinders" to have a satisfying goal. The need for goals and purposes is a basic part of the human psyche.

A sense of purpose gets us through tough times. When someone close to you dies, or when the company you've put 18 years into goes bankrupt, or when your spouse asks for a divorce, or when your house burns down—a person without a sense of purpose is more sorely tested than a person with it. At a time like that, if you can't see a good purpose in living, then you may not recover.

I have sat down and done some introspecting about my own sense of purpose in life. I have, I find, a number of purposes.

One of my purposes, because my personal midlife renaissance had such an impact on me, is to share my ideas on life-balancing. That is why I give seminars on this topic, and why I've written this book. If I can help people improve the quality of their lives, as I think mine has improved, that will make me feel very good.

Another purpose is to help businesses balance the work and the life aspects much more effectively, by looking not just to short-term profits, but also to long-term human gains for employees. I've developed quality-in-work-life programs at the companies I'm involved with. My goal is to have more energy and less stress in the daily work environment, so as to end up with higher productivity from people, because they aren't burned out and they enjoy their work environment. The result is lower turnover, happier people, higher morale, less absenteeism, and greater productivity. It works, over and over again.

Perhaps the purpose most important to me has to do with fitness. I am a speaker on wellness, a writer in triathlon magazines, and a teacher in the sports-psychology graduate psychology program at John F. Kennedy University in Orinda, California. These all tie together into one overall purpose—to be a mid-life role model in fitness after age 50.

One of the reasons for my doing 52 triathlons in one year, establishing a Guinness world record, was to prove that you can do anything you want to, no matter what your age, if you will follow the techniques described in this book. The excitement of competition can be enjoyed by people of any age, and of either sex. People think of the athlete as being a young person, but one of my dreams is to compete in the Olympics in my age class. I want to change the image of athletics as only a young person's activity. It isn't. Fitness is important at every age, and energy, aliveness, and fun don't have to be the youngster's monopoly. Why not age-class Olympics?

As a result of certain experiences, then, purpose is now a very important part of my life. Every day I think about what little steps I'm making in the direction of accomplishing my purposes.

The Purpose Self-Examination on the next pages includes some examples of human purposes that have come out of the classes I've taught. Review the list. I've left space so that you can add more if you don't find what you think should be there.

To determine how well you're doing in achieving your purposes in life, complete the exercise. Rate yourself in the interest column on a scale of 1 to 10 on the basis of how important to your sense of purpose the item is. Rate them all. Then in the next column (Involvement) rate each item on the basis of how much you think you have become involved in the purpose.

This is a little tricky. I am not asking you to rate yourself on how well you are solving the problem of world hunger, for example, but on how satisfied you are with your contribution to solving it. This is totally subjective; it is a matter of how well you are meeting your own standards. If you think you should be doing something to further a goal every day, but you actually are doing it only once a week, you might give yourself a 2 or 3 in the Involvement column. While you might be doing more toward this goal than anyone else you know, still your score of 2 or 3 would reflect your own dissatisfaction with your progress. That's what you want to measure, not any objective progress— there isn't any in the purpose department.

When you have rated all the items in the involvement column, go back and put in the variances. You may be surprised at some of the results. You may actually be doing more in some areas than you imagined, and certainly not enough—by your own standards—in others. Pick the top two or three that are important to you where the involvement is significantly lower than the interest, and think about a step or two you could take toward making them equal. Write those steps in the action column.

If you already know what your purposes are, this self-examination will show you how well you're achieving them and will suggest things you can do to speed your progress. If you haven't clarified for yourself just what your purposes in life are, this exercise will lay the foundation.

A fruitful life can let you answer "yes" to the question asked at the end:

"Did you make a difference?"

Purpose Self-Examination

Types of Purpose	Interest (+)	Involve-ment (−)	Variance (+/−)	Action
Personal Development:				
Success—Career				
—Financial				
—Personal				
Relationships				
—Marriage/ family				
—Love				
—Friends				
Happiness				
Long, enjoyable life				
Risk-taking				
Education				
Spiritual growth				
Good health				
Peace of mind				
Freedom/ independence				
Fitness				
Evolution of talents				
Answer own calling				
Other:				

Types of Purpose	Interest (+)	Involve-ment (−)	Variance (+/−)	Action
Social Problems:				
Public health				
Poverty/ unemployment				
Violence/crime				
Unwanted pregnancy				
Alcohol, other drug abuse				
Morals/ethics				
Education quality				
Leadership quality				
Discrimination in all forms				
Other:				
Public Issues:				
Nuclear disaster				
Threat of war				
Environmental problems				
Inflation/Depression				
Overpopulation				
Gun control				
Community involvement				
Other:				

Types of Purpose	Interest (+)	Involve- ment (−)	Variance (+/−)	Action
General:				
Proselytize for ideals				
Serve as a role model				
Create—Ideas				
—New products				
—Art				
—New business				
—Solutions to Problems				
Other:				

Chapter 9

BALANCE IN LIFE, WORK AND PLAY

The hardest step is that first step
But it's the road to freedom from being kept.

Now it is time to pull together all your work in this book. The result will be your master plan for the new life you are designing for yourself.

This method will put balance into your life, changing you from someone who is not satisfied with his life into someone who is having actualizing, wonderful experiences and who knows where he is going and what he is doing.

The basis of this transformation is on pages 108–9. It is called the Quality of Life Action Planner. You will be taking information from the previous chapters and transferring it to this summary. Then, using a method I have adopted from other sources, you will create plans for change, and learn how to implement them.

Considerable work is required here, but you will find it well worth while. Start by making a record of where you are now. To do that, turn back to the Quality of Life Matrix you created in Chapter 2. There you will find your scores, by area of life, along the bottom of the matrix. You will remember that these scores are totals that indicate how well your most important values are being expressed in each of the six areas of your life.

Transfer your score for each area to the space in the first column of the Action Planner on the following pages, labeled "Area of life, current rating." Put it just below each area designation. Look at my sample form on the succeeding page if you need to.

Next, in the Work row, list the major assets you think you have that are especially relevant to the Work area of your life. You can see on my sample Quality of Life Action Planner that I thought creativity and positiveness were two of my assets in the Work area. Then do the same in considering your liabilities in the Work area. If you think you lack patience, as I showed on my form, that might be a consideration.

Continue on down the Assets and Liabilities columns, entering your major assets and major liabilities in the other areas of life.

Now turn to Chapter 3 and look at the Work Preference Self Analysis. Consider your list of actions that you said you wanted to take. Choose the one or two most important ones. When you have taken these, you can come back and choose another. Enter these one or two in the Action/Goal/Steps column of the Action Planner. For example, my actions were to spend the time to better understand people's needs, and to develop a plan to promote wellness and balance in work groups.

In the next column, under "Affirmation," compose a sentence that describes what you would be willing to do to reach your goals or describes you after you have succeeded in reaching that/those goal(s). If you want to be a supervisor in your department, for example, your affirmation might be:

"I am an effective, happy supervisor," or "I am willing to develop to be an effective, happy supervisor."

If you have two goals in the work area, make an affirmation for each. The next step is to picture yourself doing the thing. Perhaps you would see yourself in the supervisor's office with your name on a desk sign there. You are smiling and self-confident. Enter a description of that picture in the column headed "Picture."

How would it feel to have achieved this goal? Gratified, proud, energetic? Write in the column headed "Feeling," several words that describe how you would feel to have attained this goal, whatever it is.

This kind of visualization is used by winning sports figures all over the world. It is one of the best ways to make small steps happen, because it creates a subconscious pull toward the goal. I have used the method for several years and have been amazed at how well it works. You can use it for any goal-oriented activity, and the following sequence for using it is always the same.

First you create an affirmation, then you picture how it will be validated, and then you imagine your feeling about it. If you refer to this goal regularly, you can look back after a period of time, perhaps three or six months later, and see marvelous results.

That's when you write in the blank "Results" column— later.

Now turn to Chapter 4 and look at your "Goals for the Coming Year" form on page 58. Fill in the Economic part of the Action Planner the way you did for Work. Enter your score from the Matrix, list your economic assets and liabilities, and transfer your most important goal(s) to the Action Planner. Write in your small steps, create your affirmation, picture, and feeling, and enter them.

Go to Chapter 5 and find your leisure action plans for the items with large variances. Transfer them to the Action Planner. Do the same with the action plans you have made in the Relationship chapter, the Spirituality chapter, and the Purpose chapter.

You have now constructed a very impressive life plan. I hope you've got the affirmations, pictures, and feelings written down. In the next three to six months, do something about those plans. Small steps. The important thing is taking some action. I do the affirmations and visualizations daily. This has been the key to setting a world athletic record and becoming president of my company.

I'm sure you have a picture in your head of what and who you are. However, other people see only your actions. Your perception of yourself is quite different from other people's percep-

Quality of Life

Area of Life + current rating	List Your Assets	List Your Liabilities	Action/Goal Small steps to take
WORK			Action/Goal:_____ _____ 1._____ 2._____ 3._____
ECONOMIC			Action/Goal:_____ _____ 1._____ 2._____ 3._____
LESIURE			Action/Goal:_____ _____ 1._____ 2._____ 3._____
RELATIONSHIP			Action/Goal:_____ _____ 1._____ 2._____ 3._____
SPIRITUAL			Action/Goal:_____ _____ 1._____ 2._____ 3._____
PURPOSE			Action/Goal:_____ _____ 1._____ 2._____ 3._____

Action Planner

Affirmation	Picture	Feeling	Result (record later)

Author's Quality of Life

Area of Life + current rating	List Your Assets	List Your Liabilities	Action/Goal Small steps to take
WORK 51	Creativity Positiveness	Not patient	Action/Goal: Spend time to better understand people's needs. 1 Develop a plan to 2. promote wellness and 3 balance in work groups
ECONOMIC 59			Action/Goal:_____ _____ 1._____ 2._____ 3._____
LESIURE 80			Action/Goal:_____ _____ 1._____ 2._____ 3._____
RELATIONSHIP 67			Action/Goal:_____ _____ 1._____ 2._____ 3._____
SPIRITUAL 59			Action/Goal:_____ _____ 1._____ 2._____ 3._____
PURPOSE 75			Action/Goal:_____ _____ 1._____ 2._____ 3._____

Action Planner (partial)

Affirmation	Picture	Feeling	Result (record later)
I am a motivating, unifying, balanced business person	Students/ employees giving me good feedback	Happy Healthy Glowing	Recently promoted to V.P. and general manager

tions of you because they are seeing what you do. To them, you are what you do. So now you have to do these steps. The old saying makes a lot of sense: Actions speak louder than words.

It is up to you to take the first step. *Just do it. Take some step!* That's the hardest part, the first one. The hardest part for me was taking that first step at the age of 47 in the back yard when I began running. But it led to setting a world record.

The purposes of this book are to help you balance your life, to give you motivation, and to help you create some self-direction. We have discussed techniques and ideas. You have to take the action. Your uniqueness, your values, make it what it will be. This workbook is a structure to help make your journey a wonderful and exciting experience.

Tear out the Action Planner and put it somewhere that you will see it daily. I carry mine in my business-planner pocket calendar. Because I carry the business planner with me all the time, I periodically look at the Action Planner, too. Sometimes I pencil in a word or two, and I update it. At the end of the year, when I do a review, I always find that I've taken almost all of the small steps I listed, or even more.

So change and grow with your personal plan. I hope you find your star, and I hope your life has the fullness that has come into mine utilizing these techniques and ideas. During *one* day a few years ago I was promoted to vice president and general manager of my company, I received a call from a reporter who informed me that my triathlon exploits had made the *Guinness Book of Records,* and I heard from the local university that I had been appointed to the school management advisory board. Wow. What a day! But I *earned* all of it by *small* steps. I will be so bold as to say you can achieve similar goals. And I hope you experience a moment similar to the one that I had in 1983. I'd like to tell you about it.

The night before the Maui Triathlon, my first big triathlon of 1983, my wife and I were in Lahaina, on Maui. By the famous banyan tree there is a place, upstairs, with a piano bar. LaVerne and I were talking about the triathlon, thinking back over the previous three years and how far we'd come, and how the next day was the big day. It was a very balmy evening, and a full moon was coming up over the mountains behind the town. The next day would be four years to the day since I had run that first half block around my back yard. And the next morning I would be on the beach with a lot of world-class triathletes. It would be a tremendous experience. My dream of being a fine athlete was being realized.

I was thinking about what a difference those four years had made, and how I had done it by just taking small steps. The night was fragrant. The view was wonderful. I was excited to be there with this woman who had changed as much as I had, who had supported me totally, and I thought about how much love we now had for each other. I was choked up. It chokes me up just to think about it now. It was a wonderful, exhilarating moment, a moment of spirituality, when there's an awareness of something special.

I tried to tell my feelings to the piano player, who had been listening to us talk. It wasn't an easy thing to convey, but he showed me he understood perfectly because he leaned toward me and said softly, "I'm going to dedicate a song to you."

And he started to play and sing "The Impossible Dream."

Bibliography

Periodicals/Courses

Age of the Runner, Runner's World Magazine Corp., 1400 Stierlin Road, Mountain View, California 94643.
American Health, American Health Partners, 80 Fifth Avenue, New York, N.Y. 10011.
Bicycle, Rodale Press, 33 E. Minor St., Emmaus, Pennsylvania 18049.
City Sports, City Sports Inc., Pier 5 South, San Francisco, California 94111.
Heartwood, California College of the Natural Healing Arts, 220 Harmony Lane, Garberville, California 95440.
John F. Kennedy University, 12 Altarinda Road, Orinda, California 94563.
The Long Search Video Series, British Broadcasting Company, London, England.
Music in Motion, P.O. Box 2688, Alameda, California 94501.
New Age Thinking, The Pacific Institute, Seattle, Washington.
The Pathway to Better Health Via Technology, William Morris, C.E.O., Control Data Corp., Minneapolis, Minn.
Runner, New Times Communication Corp., Park Avenue, New York, N.Y. 10016.
Runner's World, Runner's World Magazine Corp., 1400 Stierlin Road, Mountain View, California 94643.
Swim, R. Magnuse Enterprises Inc., 523 South 26th Road, Arlington, Virginia 22202.
Triathlon, Triathlon Magazine Limited, P.O. Box 5901, Santa Monica, California 90405.
Ultrasport, Raben Ultrasport Partners, 1 Beacon Street, Boston, Massachusetts 02105.
Unity Center, 1871 Geary Road, Walnut Creek, California.

Books

Addington, Jack Ensign; *All About Goals and How To Achieve Them,* DeVorss, Marina Del Rey, California, 1977.
Ardell, Donald B.; *High Level Wellness,* Rodale Press/Bantam, New York, 1978.
Barmash, Isadore; *The World Is Full of It,* Delacorte Press, New York, 1974.
Benson, Herbert, Dr.; *The Relaxation Response,* Morrow/Avon, New York, 1975.
Berne, Eric, M.D.; *Games People Play,* Grove Press, New York, 1974.
Bernstein, Leonard A.; *Statistics for the Executive,* Hawthorn Books, New York, 1970.
Blake, Robert R., and Jana Srygley Mouton, *Productivity, The Human Side,* AMACOM, New York, 1981.

Blanchard, Kenneth, Ph.D., and Spencer Johnson, M.D.; *The One Minute Manager,* Berkley, New York, 1981.

Bolles, Richard Nelson; *What Color Is Your Parachute,* Ten Speed Press, Berkeley, Calif., 1986.

Bolles, Richard N.; *The Three Boxes of Life and How to Get Out of Them,* Ten Speed Press, Berkeley, Calif., 1978.

Bragdon, Claude; *Yoga For You,* Knopf/Lancer, New York, 1943.

Browne, Harry; *How I Found Freedom in an Unfree World,* Macmillan, New York, 1973.

Burns, David D., M.D.; *Feeling Good,* New American Library, Bergenfield, New Jersey, 1986.

Conway, James; *Men in Midlife Crisis,* David C. Cook, Elgin, Illinois, 1978.

Cott, Alan, Dr.; *Fasting: The Ultimate Diet,* Bantam, New York, 1975.

Crosby, Phillip; *The Art of Getting Your Own Sweet Way,* McGraw Hill, New York, 1972.

Diamond, John, M.D.; *Your Body Doesn't Lie,* Harper & Row/Warner, New York, 1979.

Dickson, Paul; *The Future File,* Avon, New York, 1977.

Disney, Dorothy Cameron, and Paul Popenoe; *Can This Marriage Be Saved,* Macmillan, New York, 1972.

Drucker, Peter F.; *The Practice of Management,* Harper and Row, New York, 1954.

Drucker, Peter F.; *The Effective Executive,* Harper and Row, New York, 1966.

Drucker, Peter F.; *Managing for Results,* Harper and Row, New York, 1964.

Edwards, Sally; Triathlon, Fleet Feet Press, Sacramento, Calif., 1982.

Erhard, Warner; *Est,* Avon, New York, 1976.

Ferguson, Marilyn; *The Aquarian Conspiracy,* J. P. Tarcher, Los Angeles, Calif., 1976.

Gallwey, W. Timothy; *The Inner Game of Tennis,* Random House, New York, 1974.

Gault, Jan; *Free Time,* John Wiley & Sons, New York, 1983.

Harris, Thomas A., M.D., *I'm O.K., You're O.K.,* Harper and Row, New York, 1967.

Jampolsky, Gerald G., M.D.; *Love Is Letting Go of Fear,* Celestial Arts/Bantam, New York, 1979.

Jennings, Eugene Emerson; *Executive Stress,* Meridith, New York, 1967.

Kanin, Garson; *It Takes a Long Time to Become Young,* Doubleday, New York, 1978.

Krech, David, Richard S. Crutchfield, and Edgerton Ballachey; *Individual in Society,* McGraw Hill, New York, 1962.

Kitchens, Celebrity; *The Fresh Fruit and Vegetable Cook Book,* Berkley, New York, 1973.

Lakein, Alan; *How To Get Control of Your Time and Your Life,* David McKay, New York, 1973.

Lamott, Kenneth; *Escape from Stress,* G. P. Putnam's Sons, New York, 1975.

Larson, Bruce; *Dare To Live Now,* Zondervan, Grand Rapids, Michigan, 1967.

LeCron, Lesley M.; *Self Hypnotism,* New American Library, Bergenfield, New Jersey, 1964.

Leonard, George; *The Ultimate Athlete,* Viking/Avon, New York, 1974.

LeShan, Eda; *The Wonderful Crisis of Middle Age,* Warner, New York, 1973.

Loen, Raymond G.; *Manage More by Doing Less,* McGraw Hill, New York, 1971.

Levinson, Daniel J.; *The Seasons of a Man's Life,* Ballantine, New York, 1978.

Levinson, Harry; *Executive Stress,* Harper and Row, New York, 1964.

Lumsden, George J.; *Impact Management,* AMACOM, New York, 1979.

Lundborg, Louis B.; *The Art of Being an Executive,* Macmillan, New York, 1981.

Matthews, Clayton; *Hypnotism for the Millions,* Sherbourne, New York, 1968.

Maslow, Abraham H.; *Toward a Psychology of Being,* D. Van Nostrand, New York, 1968.

Meininger, Jut; *Transactional Analysis,* Grosset and Dunlop, New York, 1973.

Mooney, Patrick; *The Supernutrition Handbook,* Mooney, San Francisco, Calif., 1978.

Naisbitt, John; *Megatrends,* Warner, New York, 1982.

Noppel, Marjorie, and Auren Uris, *The Turned On Executive,* McGraw Hill, New York, 1976.

Peale, Norman Vincent; *A Guide to Confident Living,* Prentice Hall, New York, 1948.

Peale, Norman Vincent; *The Amazing Results of Positive Thinking,* Prentice Hall, New York, 1959.

Pelletier, Kenneth R.; *Mind As Healer, Mind As Slayer,* Dell, New York, 1977.

Pelletier, Kenneth R.; *Healthy People in Unhealthy Places,* Delacorte, New York, 1984.

Pritikin, Leonard Hofer; *Live Longer Now,* Grosset and Dunlop, New York, 1974.

Reich, Charles A.; *The Greening of America,* Random House/Bantam, New York, 1976.

Rifenbark, Richard K., and David Johnson; *How To Beat the Salary Trap,* McGraw Hill, New York, 1978.

Rogers, William; *Think,* Stein and Day, New York, 1969.

Scott, Cynthia D., and Dennis T. Jaffe; *From Burnout to Balance,* McGraw Hill, New York, 1984.

Seabury, David; *Help Yourself to Happiness,* Garden City Publishing, Garden City, New York, 1973.

Shapiro, James E.; *Ultramarathoner,* Bantam, New York, 1980.
Sheehan, Georga, Dr.; *Running and Being,* Warner, New York, 1978.
Sheehy, Gail; *Passages,* Dutton, New York, 1974.
Sheehy, Gail; *Pathfinders,* Morrow/Bantam, New York, 1981.
Spino, Mike; *Beyond Jogging,* Celestial Arts, San Francisco, Calif., 1976.
Stryker, Perrin; *The Character of the Executive,* Harper and Row, New York, 1960.
Terkel, Studs; *Working,* Pantheon/Avon, New York, 1972.
Toffler, Alvin; *Learning for Tomorrow,* Random House, New York, 1974.
Toffler, Alvin; *Future Shock,* Bantam, New York, 1974.
Toffler, Alvin; *The Third Wave,* William Morrow, New York, 1980.
Ulene, Art, Dr.; *Feeling Fine,* Ballantine, New York, 1977.
Volkman, Arthur G.; *Thoreau on Man and Nature,* Peter Pauper Press, Mount Vernon, N.Y., 1960.

Riley's Revelations

Taken together, the precepts below are my philosophy of life, based on reading hundreds of books and experiencing more than 50 years of life. It's been helpful to me and I hope it can benefit you too.

1. Develop a burning desire, based on self-knowledge of your value system, that benefits others as well as yourself.
2. Integrate good, consistent habits into your life.
3. Have written long-term and short-term goals.
4. Take small steps, and measure and reward your progress.
5. Become a student and stay one.
6. Be coachable and open.
7. Have empathy—listen, see, feel universally.
8. Have balance in life.
9. Stay close to nature.
10. Follow Pareto's 80/20 law—work smart, find your niche.
11. Use deep positive thinking—affirmations, visualizations.
12. Be focused, centered and persistent in all areas of your life.
13. Build long-term relationships in all areas of your life.
14. Have a sense of urgency—do the right thing right now.
15. Develop recovery power.
16. Always be a rookie in something.

INDEX